The
SUPERNATURAL
WOMAN

I'm A Supernatural Woman, Serving A Supernatural God, Getting Supernatural Results!

*A journey in obedience by faith and belief
that yields supernatural extreme results*

Lydia Woodson-Sloley

The Supernatural Woman
I'm a Supernatural Woman, Serving A Supernatural
God , Getting Supernatural Results

by Lydia Woodson-Sloley

Printed in the United States of America

ISBN 9781628712018

www.xulonpress.com

FOREWORD

*T*he only thing that I can explain is an inner cry that communicated to the LORD that I was at the end of my rope. I was walking in obedience to His Holy Word with everything that I had within me. I was questioning GOD asking why, in the midst of caring for a sick spouse. A word that kept me, when I didn't want to keep myself, was something so special that the LORD spoke to my heart; "Maintain your consistency while I change your circumstances." I would sit in my car listening to sermons that I had preached, listening for the revelation given by the Holy Spirit that was not written in my notes. I would listen to gospel music that spoke truth and comforted me at the same time. At times I would sit in silence asking for the strength I needed from the LORD to enter my home after a full day's work. I knew that I needed to be prepared in advance to handle my responsibilities as a wife caring for a sick spouse.

I was on the edge of being tempted to walk away from my marriage. I woke up that day and decided that I had enough. I felt that GOD was not moving

I'm a supernatural woman, serving a supernatural GOD and getting supernatural results!

fast enough for me. I felt that my consistency of serving and obeying the LORD, relative to HIS moving and changing things on my behalf, had been given ample time. I felt HE should have already moved for me. I said, "LORD, I can't do it anymore." He said to me, "You are a supernatural woman, you serve a supernatural GOD, and you get supernatural results." This statement literally shifted me into a new dimension. It was a supernatural experience as my inner man was charged with power and might. I knew that the might of the LORD was downloaded in my spirit. My circumstances didn't change, but my consistency to serve the LORD propelled me above my circumstances. I received a touch from GOD that I will never forget. The supernatural woman that GOD created me to be broke through. I had graduated to another level of faith, and the glory of the LORD was revealed. I recommitted my life to the LORD and entered into HIS rest, living, moving and having my being in CHRIST. My personal relationship with the LORD became my supernatural reality. Revelation for my present situation flowed like living water, while humility kept me in a position to be easily led by the HOLY SPIRIT with a supernatural ease.

If you have come to a place in your life, where even while serving the LORD, thinking that you can't give anymore but in your heart you love GOD, this is the book for you. It's at the end of our rope, when we are ready to give up, that HIS love continues to supernaturally stretch us to handle more through HIM. This is where our tenacity through CHRIST grants us the supernatural capacity to align with a victory

I'm a supernatural woman, serving a supernatural GOD and getting supernatural results!

that's already ours. You are invited to partake in this prophetic and poetic extreme journey, into the supernatural realities of everyday living through CHRIST.

Enjoy, grow, and flow!

Reverend Lydia Woodson-Sloley

ABOUT THE AUTHOR

*L*ydia received Jesus Christ as her personal Lord and Savior in 1982. She was ordained an Elder and called to the office of a Prophet in 1997. Lydia was elevated to the Apostolic office on May 29, 2011 at Holy City Faith & Deliverance Center of Love under the leadership of Apostle Callie Mae Jasper. The Lord blessed Lydia with a unique gift. This poetic-prophetic gift has opened doors and blessed the lives of many nationally as well as internationally. Lydia successfully completed the National Broadcasting School, where her radio broadcast, *Life In its Poetic Form* was born.

Lydia serves as host of the *Supernatural Woman Radio* broadcast, airing on WSKY, Asheville, NC, WWNL Pittsburgh, PA, WFAM, Augusta, GA, WIJD AM and WIJD FM, Mobile, AL, and KWDF, Alexandria, LA. . Lydia recently released her CD called "The Supernatural Woman." This CD can be downloaded from the Supernatural Woman website www.swoman.info

A published author, Lydia's last book, *The Fountain of Youth Called Truth*, offers women ten

I'm a supernatural woman, serving a supernatural GOD and getting supernatural results!

supernatural life-preserving beauty secrets found in the Word of God. Lydia has also authored five books of poetry; *Inspirational Insights, Relationships, Challenging Experiences, Knowing Yourself through Christ* and *Understanding Our Emotions*.

A certified independent cable television producer, Lydia writes, produces, and directs her own television broadcast, *Life In its Poetic Form*, an inspirational talk show, design to inspire, encourage, and motivate its viewers to accept the challenges of everyday living. Lydia, a "Certified Image Consultant," established the "Life Empowerment Workshops." These workshops teach life skills from the inside out and are highly praised by schools, churches, correctional facilities, shelters for battered women, teen programs, and corporations. She is the founder of the Poetry Empowerment Workshops. These workshops offer an invitation, to the hearts of other writers to speak through poetry. Lydia has written for two Christian newspapers, the *Love Express* and the *Christian Times* newspapers in New York City.

Lydia, is a profound anointed supernatural woman who has ministered nationally as well as internationally preaching and teaching the Word of God. She is presently founder, Apostle, and Senior Pastor of Life In Its Poetic Form Christian Ministries Inc. in Brooklyn, New York, where storms are calmed and inner issues are settled.

I'm a supernatural woman, serving a supernatural GOD and getting supernatural results!

THE SUPERNATURAL WOMAN

The most important thing to know about the supernatural woman is that she is not limited by time. Although she treasures her time, her eternal perspective positions her to abide in her Christ likeness where supernatural results automatically manifest. This is where she experiences proven supernatural victorious strategies, demonstrated by the living WORD OF GOD that's already been tested and tried by her supernatural living GOD.

The supernatural woman knows that the mind of CHRIST in her supersedes her natural mind. This establishes her supernatural reality, whereby yielding to the mind of CHRIST within her, is where she discovers HIS supernatural peace. GOD'S supernatural peace is able to sustain her until the storm clears or the answer is revealed. She knows, by the SPIRIT OF THE LIVING GOD, that there is no situation or circumstance that manifest in her life that her living SAVIOR is not already aware of.

The supernatural woman lives within a living salvation, constantly discovering what's already

I'm a supernatural woman, serving a supernatural GOD and getting supernatural results!

been done in the finished work of her LORD and SAVIOR JESUS CHRIST. Her supernatural reality of this living salvation is where her way of escape already exists. She knows that within this living salvation, living answers to her prayers already exist. The answer is supernaturally waiting to attach itself to her call, because the LORD has already heard her cry.

Obedience to her living GOD is the supernatural woman's way of life. This is her way of saying, "JESUS, I love you." Even in times of great pain, persecution, and self-justification, where her flesh tells her, "You have a right to get even," she will obey her living SAVIOR'S supernatural voice. Once again, she knows that she serves a supernatural GOD, getting supernatural results, and she waits patiently for revelation, coupled with the manifestation of her victory.

The supernatural woman lives in holiness. She knows that is the only way to have full access to the presence of her living SAVIOR. HE tells her to "be holy as I am holy." Her holy desire to be like her living SAVIOR, positions her to operate in HIS image and HIS likeness. The supernatural woman values the price that HE paid on Calvary and dares to walk in HIS resurrection power. The supernatural woman does not live in mediocrity; she lives in power and authority because of the intimacy that she has with her living SAVIOR. If she has to remind herself moment by moment, she will boldly refuse to serve wicked influences.

The supernatural woman has supernatural discernment. She is alert relative to the immediacy of her surroundings. Being easily led by the Holy Spirit, she is conscious of living in the moment where the fullness of life exists rather than living in her past rehearsing life's drama. The supernatural woman never loses her identity in the wilderness. Even when she can't trace her living SAVIOR, she still trusts HIM. When she says, "Let go and let GOD," this is a real place of freedom for her. She lives in the sweet communion of the Holy Spirit.

The supernatural woman surrenders thoughts that violate the will of GOD for her life. She will rebuke her own self, reminding herself that there is no good thing in her flesh and her supernatural GOD will withhold no good thing from her as she walks upright before HIM. Alive in CHRIST, for the supernatural woman, is that place where living, moving, and having her being in her GOD is her life. This has become her supernatural reality. The supernatural woman's objective is to bring pleasure to her CREATOR, the MAKER of heaven and earth. She knows that when the CREATOR gets pleasure out of HIS creation, she is walking in her preordained purpose and destiny; for she knows that her steps are ordered by the LORD.

The supernatural woman has closed the gap between hesitation and Godly revelation through obedience. She has a keen sense of awareness and discernment and makes every attempt to nullify demonic influences that come from the enemy's camp. I can do all things through CHRIST is her supernatural living reality. This is her summation relative to daily victorious living secret revelatory strategies that was given to her before the foundations of the world.

I'm a supernatural woman, serving a supernatural GOD and getting supernatural results!

I'm a supernatural woman, serving a supernatural GOD and getting supernatural results!

Reverend Lydia Woodson-Sloley

TABLE OF CONTENTS

Supernatural Love Letter 15
The Supernatural Power of a Life Laid Down . . . 21
Supernatural Holy Satisfaction 29
Supernatural Extreme Faith 39
Supernatural Sheep that the Wolf Can't Keep . . . 50
The Supernatural Momentum of the LORD 60
Supernatural Living Is HOLY GHOST Driven. . . 67
The Supernatural Force of Righteousness 74
Supernatural Holy Revelation Exposes
All Imitation 83
A Transformed You Living in the
Supernatural New 93
Supernaturally Speaking, No Permission
Is Needed 101

I'm a supernatural woman, serving a supernatural GOD and getting supernatural results!

Chapter 1

Supernatural Love Letter

Song of Solomon 2:10
My lover spoke and said to me, "Arise, my darling, my beautiful one, and come with me."

The Prophetic–Poetic Word
Come away MY beloved is a supernatural invitation, whereby, I ignite in you the image of ME that I created you to be.

It's that place in ME says the LORD where you encounter MY presence.

It's that place in ME where I have already made you free.

Come away MY Beloved; don't pull away from ME in the Spirit.

I long for you more that you will ever know says the LORD,

as I gently woo you, it's obedience that will cause you to hear it.

There is an all-points bulletin that has been released for MY Beloved,
you in ME and I in you is like a hand that fits in a glove.

The angels are on assignment to minster to your needs. Did I not say that I would never leave you or forsake you?
You have access to the incorruptible seed.

Come away MY Beloved; come into MY embrace,
you will find MY supernatural peace in our intimate space.

Supernatural Love Letter to the Supernatural Woman

I tell you this day, says the TRUE and LIVING GODprepare yourselves for a close encounter with ME in the living room of MY KINGDOM. Every time that MY BELOVED comes to ME, I'VE supernaturally enticed you with MY goodness and mercy that follows you every day or you have learned to run into MY arms in times of trouble. Either way, the supernatural side effects of our encounter yield supernatural results.

There are undiscovered places in ME that I long to introduce you to. Every time you come away with ME into the secret place of the MOST HIGH, I will indulge you into a new level of freedom that is already available to you, says the LORD. I will never disappoint you, says the LORD; there is an overwhelming joy in MY presence that will make you secure in MY love. Come away, MY Beloved.

The HOLY SCRIPTURES testify in ***Psalm 21:6-7*** *"in the presence of the LORD, there is joy. Surely you have granted him eternal blessings and made Him glad with the joy of your presence. For the king trusts in the LORD; through the unfailing love of the Most High he will not be shaken."* Oh, there is a shaking taking place in the earth, says the LORD, and the only way that you will not be shaken is in MY love. As I rock you in MY arms, you won't be disturbed when things are shaking around you.

There are new songs that I long to hear that I'VE already placed in your heart, says the LORD.

I'm a supernatural woman, serving a supernatural GOD and getting supernatural results!

I created you to worship ME. Don't miss glorifying ME; it ignites the new song. Coming away with ME, says the LORD, allows ME to bring you into places in ME that will quiet your fiercest storm. This is not a season to pull away from ME in the spirit. Some of you act like you can't hear MY voice when I gently correct you or gently lead you. Let MY SPIRIT lead your spirit. Stop letting your soul lead your spirit. When your soul leads your spirit, it gives power to your flesh. This creates instability in your emotions. How dare you long for something more than you long for ME, says the LORD.

I created you to live in the spirit, where by faith you receive instructions from ME. Your spirit will control your soul and silence your flesh. You can't date ME with your flesh; you can only become one with ME in the spirit. Come away, MY Beloved. When you come willingly before you have to surrender, the light of MY love will search your spirit. I will seek out in you for you and show you what's holding you back from seeking ME and loving ME more. I will cause you to supernaturally interact with MY love.

The HOLY SCRIPTURES testify in *Proverbs 20:27: The lamp of the LORD searches the spirit of a man; it searches out his inmost being.* I'M preparing MY glorious church for whom I'M coming back for to be without spot or wrinkle. I can bring light into your darkness and reveal to you the real you that looks like ME, says the LORD. Come away, MY Beloved; don't pull away from ME when I'M calling you.

The world has the energized bunny, but when you are with ME says the LORD I will energize you with MY supernatural honey. I'M sweeter than the honey in the honeycomb. There is an all-points bulletin out in the spirit says the LORD for those whom MY FATHER placed in MY hand, and not one of them is lost. At the right place and at the right time within time, they will hear MY call and receive MY supernatural invitation to come away. Before the foundations of the world, it was preordained to be, I in them and they in ME … oh how close we can be, says the LORD.

The HOLY SCRIPTURES testify in ***John 17:20, 23:*** *"My prayer is not for them alone. I pray also for those who will believe in me through their message, that all of them may be one, Father, just as you are in me and I am in you. May they also be in us so that the world may believe that you have sent me. I have given them the glory that you gave me that they may be one as we are one: I in them and you in me. May they be brought to complete unity to let the world know that you sent me and have loved them even as you have loved me.* I tell you this day, says the TRUE and LIVING GODthe more you take ME up on MY supernatural invitation to come away; the more others will want what you have. The ME in you is what they are seeking. I will empower you as MY supernatural woman with MY presence says the LORD, and souls will be multiplied in MY Kingdom.

Finally, I'M in love with MY beloved. I love you so much, says the LORD that I have provided supernatural assistance whereby I send the angels to minister to the heirs of salvation. I love you so much, says the LORD, that when MY love flows through you, it affects your whole house where the seed of the righteous is saved. Come away MY beloved with the one who will never forsake you. You are MY seed, and I'M your imperishable seed. I was planted as the living WORD in the living womb of a woman by the overshadowing of the HOLY SPIRIT in order to bring new birth to you. You are MY seed, and I'M your imperishable seed. The HOLY SCRIPTURES testify in *1 Peter 1:23: "For you have been born again, not of perishable seed, but of imperishable, through the living and enduring word of God."*

Come away MY Beloved into MY everlasting love. Anyone planted in ME will experience MY eternal life and eternal love. Come away MY Beloved; come into MY embrace where you will find MY supernatural peace in our intimate space. Come away MY Beloved; hold on to MY unchanging hand and walk with ME in the spirit. You will experience levels of intimacy in ME like never before. Come away MY Beloved you are MY supernatural woman.

Chapter 2

THE SUPERNATURAL POWER OF A LIFE LAID DOWN

John 10:17–18.

The reason my Father loves me is that I lay down my life only to take it up again. 18No one takes it from me, but I lay it down of my own accord. I have authority to lay it down and authority to take it up again. This command I received from my Father.

The Poetic-Prophetic Word

It takes commitment based on wisdom and revelation of destiny foreknown,

to supernaturally lay your life down in order to reign with Christ.

There is supernatural power to decree what you can't see;

even while going through the storms of life, you never forget Calvary's price.

I'm a supernatural woman, serving a supernatural GOD and getting supernatural results!

Even in the midst of hearing those who cheered ME on, says the LORD,
I could also see those who are trying to take ME under.
We must be careful of our neediness for man and not God.
The supernatural power of a life laid down is where the righteous resist the enemy's plunder.

In this season of supernatural aggression,
we must never forget what the LORD has already done.
He had the supernatural power to lay HIS life down and picked it up again
because there was never a partnership between holiness and sin.

The Supernatural Power of a Life Laid Down

The LORD is saying to HIS supernatural women that we will be empowered to reign with HIM and have access to HIS foreknowledge, revelation and wisdom about our destiny and purpose, based on the level of commitment that we are willing to make by laying our lives down to follow HIM. Based on our commitment relative to living a surrendered life, thereby will the LORD release HIS wisdom and revelation in order to inform us of things to come that HE'S already done. In other words the LORD is saying that anything we refuse to die to will rob us of what HE wants to bring us into. The supernatural power of a life laid down demonstrates love, forgiveness, drinks of the living water, wins souls, embraces the Kingdom of GOD, lives in CHRIST, walking in the HIS finished work and is led by the Spirit of GOD.

On our journey to becoming a supernatural woman we must be clear about the category that we fit in. Is our life laid down, laid up, or on lay-away? The supernatural power of a life laid down for CHRIST positions the righteous in a supernatural authority that the enemy does not have access to. Although the devil has power, he has no authority. All power and authority was given to our LORD AND SAVIOR JESUS CHRIST. Based on the level of commitment that we are willing to make by laying our lives down to follow HIM, we will be empowered to reign with HIM and have access to HIS foreknowledge, revelation, and wisdom about our destiny and purpose.

I'm a supernatural woman, serving a supernatural GOD and getting supernatural results!

The HOLY SCRIPTURES testify that the FATHER'S love, plan and authority were involved when HE gave the command to HIS SON to lay HIS life down. The account picks up in ***John 10:17, 18:*** *The reason my Father loves me is that I lay down my life only to take it up again. No one takes it from me, but I lay it down of my own accord. I have authority to lay it down and authority to take it up again. This command I received from my Father."*

Obediently, JESUS CHRIST chose to die, no one had the power to take HIS life. HE said I have the power to lay it down and to pick it up again. So what is the LORD saying to us? The supernatural power of a life laid down has access to the supernatural wisdom of GOD, and we get same results that HE did when HE laid HIS life down.

Supernatural Tips for the Supernatural Woman

Whatever you have to lay down in life to follow CHRIST, you pick up the supernatural power to overcome through CHRIST.

A life laid down is a life that has supernatural instant access to power and revelation for your present situation. A life laid down walks in the answers to life, which is the wisdom of GOD being revealed that brings release and relief. The LORD is telling us there is a level of obedience that releases the power of HIS supernatural authority that overrides whatever that devil tries to do. The supernatural power of a life laid down has the power to operate in realms of supernatural authority. When our lives are laid down in

I'm a supernatural woman, serving a supernatural GOD and getting supernatural results!

CHRIST, we are never concerned about our personal ability because we know that the power of CHRIST is at work in us.

When our life is laid up, we live in layers of drama and confusion. What we don't let go of demonically grips us. When we are laid up in confusion and drama, our life is lockdown by the enemy. When we are on demonic lockdown, it's because we are not fully submitted to GOD; therefore, we can't resist or rebuke that devil through CHRIST. It's where we feel like we are stuck and there is no movement relative to our personal progress in life. It's where we had the audacity to expect progress but we are not making any progress. Is your life laid up?

A life on lay-away is a life that keeps returning to sin and keeps trying to make a down payment on sinful behavior through works, even in the church. Are we trying to serve GOD while living in sin? It's just like going back to the store to make a down payment for something that you would like to eventually own. In CHRIST our lives are already stamped paid in full. A life on lay-away forgot how to steal away with JESUS and sup with the SAVIOR. Holiness has no partnership with sin. Is your life on lay-away? The supernatural power of a life laid down has access to the supernatural wisdom of GOD, and we get results as when CHRIST laid HIS life down.

The Apostle Paul, who laid down his life to follow CHRIST, found himself in a situation where on his journey he encountered the intelligentsia, know-it-alls, who because of their lack of humility, destroyed their power to believe and receive. They tried to oppose Paul.

I'm a supernatural woman, serving a supernatural GOD and getting supernatural results!

The HOLY SCRIPTURES testify in *1 Corinthians 2:1-5: (the Apostle Paul is speaking) When I came to you, brothers, I did not come with eloquence or superior wisdom as I proclaimed to you the testimony about God. For I resolved (determined) to know nothing while I was with you except Jesus Christ and him crucified. I came to you in weakness and fear, and with much trembling. My message and my preaching were not with wise and persuasive words, but with a demonstration of the Spirit's power, so that your faith might not rest on men's wisdom, but on God's power.*

I've learned something in my walk with GOD: as a supernatural woman, humility, wisdom, and kindness will dismantle the enemy's agenda. The Apostle Paul's life was so laid down, even in the midst of Paul's own fears, the Spirit of GOD rested on him to communicate to those enemies of the cross. Paul was saying; don't let your faith rest on the wisdom of men, but on the power of GOD. Only a life laid down in CHRIST will know the difference. Is your life laid down, laid up, or on lay-away?

Just as I walked towards Calvary, says the LORD, preparing to lay MY life down and picking it up again, there were haters and believers, and through the foreknowledge of MY FATHER I could see who HE had placed into MY hands as well as those who were enemies of the cross. I tell you this day says the TRUE and LIVING GOD, the supernatural power of a life laid down allows you to discern those who smile in your face while stabbing you in the back in the moment, as well as empowering you to resist the enemy so that he is no longer able to steal, kill, and destroy your life.

I'm a supernatural woman, serving a supernatural GOD and getting supernatural results!

Supernatural Tip for the Supernatural Woman

The LORD is saying to us that the supernatural power of a life laid down can master all atmospheres. There are something's you must never stop to address, just keep moving until you come through the other side.

Let ME remind you, says the LORD, some opposition that many are experiencing today is a direct result of sowing disobedience and reaping disobedience. That's the law of sowing and reaping. What you put out is what you will get back. The Apostle Paul said in *Galatians 6:7: "Do not be deceived: God cannot be mocked. A man reaps what he sows."*

There is also some opposition that I allow, says the LORD, as a decoy to make the enemy think that he's got you. The supernatural reality is … it's a trap for him. Just when that devil thinks he's got you, what he meant for evil, I, the LORD, will turn it around for your good. There was nothing that Satan could do to ME that could withstand the supernatural outcome of what was preordained to manifest. MY walk to Calvary, says the LORD, was a demonstration of hidden supernatural outcomes that are now available to true believers.

The HOLY SCRIPTURES testify in *1Corinthians 2:8 that none of the rulers of this age understood it, for if they had, they would not have crucified the Lord of glory.* Although MY enemies could see the cross, they couldn't see MY resurrection. Although your enemies can see where you are headed they can't see what I'M about to give to you says the LORD.

I'm a supernatural woman, serving a supernatural GOD and getting supernatural results!

Supernatural Tips for a Supernatural Woman...

Be careful of our neediness for men and not for GOD. They don't have the capacity to handle the weight of what you believe GOD for. For clergy, it's good to have an armor bearer, but they can't bear the responsibility of your capacity. Do not lean too hard on others; it will cut off your hearing and the leading of the HOLY SPIRIT in your lives.

As I headed towards Calvary says the LORD, there was no man that I could depend on. The capacity of MY responsibility was in MY FATHER'S plans, says the LORD. What we discussed in the plan of salvation before the foundations of the world, had to be supernaturally processed in the flesh by the SPIRIT of GOD through the SON, in order for the supernatural reality of MY preordained victory to manifest and be handed over to the righteous.

The HOLY SCRIPTURES testify in *1 Corinthians 15:57: "But thanks be to God! He gives us the victory through our Lord Jesus Christ."* The supernatural power of a life laid down has the capacity to take the victory that has already been given. The level of commitment that we are willing to make by laying our lives down to follow HIM, will be the level with which we are empowered to reign with HIM and have access to HIS foreknowledge, revelation, and wisdom about our destiny and purpose of things to come, that HE'S already done. I'M A VICTORIOUS SUPERNATURAL WOMAN

Chapter 3

SUPERNATURAL HOLY SATISFACTION

Psalm 91:14 -16

Because he loves me, says the LORD, I will rescue him; I will protect him, for he acknowledges my name. He will call upon me, and I will answer him; I will be with him in trouble, I will deliver him and honor him. With long life will I satisfy him and show him my salvation.

The Poetic-Prophetic Word
Thirsting after righteousness is a supernatural satisfier, says the LORD,
that connects the righteous to a continuous flow of living water.
It's where what already exists for the righteous has a revelatory release,
that's loaded with power and has already broken through the enemy's border.

I'm a supernatural woman, serving a supernatural GOD and getting supernatural results!

Supernatural holy satisfaction is where holiness establishes levels of dependency,
when the righteous supernaturally surrender.
It's that hidden place in CHRIST that makes a hardened heart supernaturally tender.

It's where in our everyday decisions the SPIRIT OF THE LORD is allowed to reign,
It's that supernatural place where the revelation of our pain reveals our gain.

Supernatural holy satisfaction,
is where the righteous are led to stored up treasures that don't rot or rust.
It's where rewards from obedience are bestowed upon those who dare to surrender to blind trust.

Supernatural Holy Satisfaction

SUPERNATURAL HOLY SATISFACTION is crucial, for many are coming to the end of their rope, because nothing in this world can satisfy what the soul is seeking for. SUPERNATURAL HOLY SATISFACTION means to exist in the ultimate state of surrender whereby your trusting in ME says the LORD, is not interrupted by visual circumstances. Supernaturally trusting in ME, says the LORD, solidifies your needs being met beyond your comprehension or capacity to understand. This means by faith, never doubting, that every void in your life is already fulfilled. It's where we have to live in the now, in order to have access to the already.

SUPERNATURAL HOLY SATISFACTION is a sacred place where supernatural fulfillment is experienced as we wait patiently on the LORD, for the full manifestation of what it is we believe for. This means that we have made a conscious decision not to look to anyone or anything to fulfill any need, which only the LORD, the MAKER of heaven and earth has already fulfilled. SUPERNATURAL HOLY SATISFACTION is a sacred place where we have access to what already exist for us.

Supernatural Tips for the Supernatural Woman

Supernatural holy satisfaction for the supernatural woman is that place in CHRIST, where every void is filled and every need is met. It's that place where we

I'm a supernatural woman, serving a supernatural GOD and getting supernatural results!

are positioned in CHRIST where the promise of our hearts' desires awaits us.

The HOLY SCRIPTURES testify in **Psalm 91** about the secret place of the MOST HIGH. The LORD is drawing our attention to where the psalmist assures and confirms that the Godly, those who trust in GOD will receive the promises of GOD. *Psalm 91:14-16: because he loves me, says the LORD, I will rescue him; I will protect him, for he acknowledges my name. He will call upon me, and I will answer him; I will be with him in trouble, I will deliver him and honor him. With long life will I satisfy him and show him my salvation.* There are seven "I will's" in these two verses. The LORD says I will do, which means HE already has the capacity to carry it out or fulfill our request. SUPERNATURAL HOLY SATISFACTION is a sacred place where supernatural fulfillment is experienced as we wait patiently on the LORD for the full manifestation of what it is we believe for. This means that whatever the need or the situation, the LORD already has the answer to the question or the solution to the problem in place. I will show him MY salvation. Salvation means deliverance, rescue, recovery, and escape. SUPERNATURAL HOLY SATISFACTION has supernatural side effects from living a surrendered life through our LORD and SAVIOR JESUS CHRIST.

I want you to pay close attention, says the LORD. Unpredictable storms and weather patterns tell their own story. Many failed to understand the sign of the times, for truly judgment is in the earth. Many things have shifted, and we will witness in days to come where things have landed, even in our own lives,

I'm a supernatural woman, serving a supernatural GOD and getting supernatural results!

says the LORD. The supernatural divine alignment, relative to how things have been preordained to exist, will make its adjustments, whether we are ready or not, says The TRUE and LIVING GOD

In other words the LORD is saying HE is not waiting for us to move or change before HE decides to move or make a change.

In MY supernatural attempts to get the attention of un-surrendered hearts through MY HOLY WORD from generation to generation by extending MY grace to those who don't even know that I'M trying to get their attention, many are still crying out to the false idols of their own addictions by trusting in anything and everything but ME says the LORD. SUPERNATURAL HOLY SATISFACTION can only be found in ME says the LORD.

The HOLY SCRIPTURES testify in the book of Jeremiah about the Prophet Jeremiah who preached about the judgment of GOD and who, in the pursuit of his divine vocation, was known as a fiery preacher of righteousness. His oracles have lost none of their power with the passing of the centuries. In exposing the kings of Judah who failed to obey GOD, the HOLY SCRIPTURES reveal a portion of what the LORD spoke through the Prophet Jeremiah. The account picks up in ***Jeremiah 8:4-7:*** *"Say to them, this is what the LORD says: 'When men fall down, do they not get up? When a man turns away, does he not return? Why then have these people turned away? Why does Jerusalem always turn away? They cling to deceit; they refuse to return. I have listened attentively, but they do not say what is right. No*

I'm a supernatural woman, serving a supernatural GOD and getting supernatural results!

33

one repents of his wickedness, saying, "What have I done?" Each pursues his own course like a horse charging into battle. Even the stork in the sky knows her appointed seasons, and the dove, the swift and the thrush observe the time of their migration. But my people do not know the requirements of the LORD."

Even in the body of CHRIST, the church, because of sin, coupled with the lack repentance that destroys faith and trust, Christians sit in seats of dissatisfaction and despair because they refuse to acknowledge the requirements of the LORD. Today, I come to tell you, says the TRUE and LIVING GOD, there is a way of escape for true believers, those who dare to trust ME beyond their comprehension. It's that place where they stop trying to figure out how I'M going to do it or even why they deserve it, while wrestling with demonic influences who say they can't have it. Today, I invite you into a realm of SUPERNATURAL HOLY SATISFACTION, says the LORD.

The LORD is saying, in spite of what the devil is trying to stop, he does not have the power to block what I'M trying to get to you. There is no border or blockade in the devils camp, says the LORD, which has not already been broken through. The only things that are holding us back are those things that we won't let go of. There is revelation for every situation in the atmosphere right now. What's already designated for MY supernatural woman is expedited when she surrenders to MY SUPERNATURAL HOLY SATISFACTION.

SUPERNATURAL HOLY SATISFACTION means to exist in the ultimate state of surrender whereby our trusting in the LORD is not interrupted by visual circumstances. Supernaturally trusting in ME, says the LORD, solidifies our needs being met beyond our comprehension or capacity to understand. This means we believe by faith, never doubting that every void in our life is already fulfilled. Remember we have to live in the now, in order to have access to the already.

In the book of *John, Chapter 4* I told the woman at the well that she had five husbands and the one she was with was not hers. I told her that I AM LIVING WATER, says the LORD. She went from relationship to relationship and never found satisfaction, just like many of us who go from relationship to relationship looking for satisfaction. Anything that we have a relationship with, to include, people, places, things, or even animals will never be able to satisfy our soul or give us living water. MY conversation continued with the woman at the well where MY HOLY SCRIPTURES testify in *John 4:13-14: "Jesus answered, everyone who drinks this water will be thirsty again, but whoever drinks the water I give him will never thirst. Indeed, the water I give him will become in him a spring of water welling up to eternal life."*

The danger is that people are trying to fulfill their thirst with things that I created, says the LORD. I created people, places, and things. Anything that I created, says the LORD, cannot supernaturally fulfill a thirsty soul. Only the one who created the soul can fulfill its thirst, says the TRUE and LIVING GOD Every outside attraction will be a distraction if you want it more than ME says the LORD. The LIVING

WATER that I AM is, is the only thing that can bring SUPERNATURAL HOLY SATISFACTION to your soul. It's the fountain that never runs dry. LIVING WATER, living in you, produces a spring of living water welling up, so the water in the well never runs dry.

LIVING WATER is so powerful it sprung up out of hell and deliver eternal life to every believer. The LIVING WATER that overpowered hell is the same LIVING WATER in you that can take the hell out of you. BE ALERT … The very thing that we are thirsting after, can take us under water and cause us to drown in our circumstances. The same LIVING WATER you drink through MY HOLY WORD is the same LIVING WATER that you will see face-to-face in eternal life, says the TRUE and LIVING GOD. SUPERNATURAL HOLY SATISFACTION must become our main attraction.

The Supernatural Tip for the Supernatural Woman

The revelation of the LORD does not have to excuse itself in order to break through enemy territory. It supernaturally overrides the enemy's agenda. The revelation of the Lord provides SUPERNATURAL HOLY SATISFACTION that will cause us to surrender our opinion for GOD'S perspective.

WE need LIVING WATER to defeat and over-come our enemies. LIVING WATER living inside of us gives us the power to overcome the enemy. If the LIVING WATER is not living in us, the devil will influence us to argue all day long. We will be

I'm a supernatural woman, serving a supernatural GOD and getting supernatural results!

looking for revenge because we are dry and frustrated inside. Only if LIVING WATER is living in us, can we overcome evil with good.

The HOLY SCRIPTURES testify about the Apostle Paul speaking in **Romans 12:17-21**: *"Do not repay anyone evil for evil. Be careful to do what is right in the eyes of everybody. If it is possible, as far as it depends on you, live at peace with everyone. Do not take revenge, my friends, but leave room for God's wrath, for it is written: "It is mine to avenge; I will repay," says the Lord. On the contrary: If your enemy is hungry, feed him; if he is thirsty, give him something to drink. In doing this, you will heap burning coals on his head. Do not be overcome by evil, but overcome evil with good".*

SUPERNATURAL HOLY SATISFACTION keeps us in a position where GOD tenderizes our hearts. Let me use the example of a meat tenderizer: both the seasonings and the mallet. The seasonings blended together with perfection can make any meat dish excite our taste buds, but if the meat is tough and hard to chew, it's not only hard to digest but often left on the plate. The same is with the heart of man. If the heart is not surrendered, it's impossible to be tenderized. What comes out of a hard heart, which is exposed by the mouth, if not seasoned with grace, often leaves a bitter taste. Then the mallet of repercussion, often from the lack of repentance, applies pressure to our everyday lives.

The HOLY SCRIPTURES testify in **Jeremiah 17:9-10**: *"The heart is deceitful above all things and beyond cure. Who can understand it? "I the LORD search the heart and examine the mind, to reward a man*

I'm a supernatural woman, serving a supernatural GOD and getting supernatural results!

according to his conduct, according to what his deeds deserve." A heart surrendered to SUPERNATURAL HOLY SATISFACTION is a heart that is not deceitful. Surrender makes our heart supernaturally tender; it's where our trust in GOD solidifies our needs being met and voids being filled. Supernatural holy satisfaction is where holiness establishes levels of dependency, when the righteous supernaturally surrender. It's that hidden place in CHRIST, that makes a harden heart supernaturally tender. The LORD is telling us that there is supernatural activity that is in operation when we allow HIM to reign in our decisions. What the devil meant for evil, HE will turn around for our good. There is supernatural revelation that is revealed to us in our pain that provides a way of escape for us and becomes our gain when we remain holy while going through the trials of life. The LORD is saying that there is a way out of every demonic trap. What HE reveals to us, in our surrendered holy state, is the key to our freedom, and if we obey it, our gain is both natural and supernatural. Our brokenness in surrender tells HIM that we could not work it out, even financially, and we need HIS original plan of action and not our distraction to the enemy's attraction.

Supernatural Tips for the Supernatural Woman

When the enemy's attractions become our distractions, there is no satisfaction. Be alert, it could look good, sound good, taste good, feel good and smell good but it's no good.

I'm a supernatural woman, serving a supernatural GOD and getting supernatural results!

Chapter 4

SUPERNATURAL EXTREME FAITH

Matthew 9:29
Then he touched their eyes and said,
"According to your faith will it be done to
you"; and their sight was restored.

The Poetic-Prophetic Word
Average is not part of MY creation says the LORD;
everything that I created is supernaturally extreme.
Don't equate what you see with your natural eye,
with what I'VE already done that's supernaturally unseen.

I'M inviting you into the supernatural realm of extreme faith,
where before the foundations of the world, what I said would come into existence.
Supernatural extreme faith is a realm,
where there is no room for the lack of repentance.

I'm a supernatural woman, serving a supernatural GOD and getting supernatural results!

In the realm of supernatural extreme faith, time doesn't exist.
Wickedness has no power to block the blessing of the righteous;
they know how to make the devil flee, based on how they resist.

Supernatural extreme faith is the ultimate point,
to which the activity of MY HOLY WORD is carried out.
When I said let there be light,
it was a holy supernatural extreme discussion where doubt was locked out.
I'M calling for supernatural extreme faith where unlimited supply exist,
It's where the exceeding and abundant blessing will never be missed.

Supernatural Extreme Faith

Prophetically speaking supernatural extreme faith is a constant engaged communication by faith with the TRUE and LIVING GOD. It is where the supernatural reality of partaking of his divine nature empowers us to believe beyond our own comprehension with ease and in peace. Supernatural extreme faith is where supernatural results manifest. Hear with your inner ear.

I tell you, says the LORD, nothing that I have already done or will continue to do for MY righteous remnant is average. There is nothing common about SUPERNATURAL EXTREME FAITH. As I grant you the capacity to believe, I supernaturally broaden the Mind of Christ in you, relative to the level of faith that you allow yourself to step into. SUPERNATURAL EXTREME FAITH is a realm without measure. When the two blind men who approached ME, says the LORD, I said, "According to your faith it will be done to you," I was saying that I know that you are excited about what you heard, but do you believe that it can happen to you? SUPERNATURAL EXTREME FAITH requires supernatural agreement.

MY HOLY SCRIPTURES testify in *Matthew 9:27-29: "As Jesus went on from there, two blind men followed him, calling out, 'Have mercy on us, Son of David!' When he had gone indoors, the blind men came to him, and he asked them, 'Do you believe that I am able to do this?' 'Yes, Lord,' they replied. Then he touched their eyes and said, 'According to your faith will it be done to you'; and their sight was*

I'm a supernatural woman, serving a supernatural GOD and getting supernatural results!

restored." I tell you this day says the LORD, the word according means to agree, a state in which things are in harmony with each other. I was asking the blind men, are you in agreement with ME based on what you believe that I can do? I asked this because it is possible that you can believe that I can do this, but not believe that it can be done for you. When they gave ME that SUPERNATURAL YES, says the LORD, it catapulted their faith into the SUPERNAURAL EXTREME and their sight manifested.

Supernatural Tips for the Supernatural Woman

It's not what you feel; it's not what you see, but it's what you believe. Supernatural extreme faith is a realm without measure. Be it unto you according to your faith.

In the realm of SUPERNATURAL EXTREME FAITH, follow ME closely, says the LORD, just like the two blind men. They couldn't see ME, but they followed ME. You can't see ME but you believe that I exist…The more of MY presence that you desire, says the LORD, the more I expose to you that which I'VE already done for you. SUPERNATURAL EXTREME FAITH is where you believe in ME until you see what I see.

SUPERNATURAL EXTREME FAITH can never be measured with the natural eye. The natural eye only has the capacity to see what already exists. There is an unseen realm of SUPERNATURAL abundance and assistance whereby every aspect of your life relative to divine protection and divine release is already made available to you says the LORD. MY objective

I'm a supernatural woman, serving a supernatural GOD and getting supernatural results!

in this hour is to get my remnant in a place where they align with the answer that has already been released. According to your faith it will be done unto you.

The HOLY SCRIPTURES testify, says the LORD, that the Prophet Elisha asked ME to open up the eyes of his servant to see the supernatural angelic assistance relative to the opposition that faced them. There is always more supernatural assistance, unseen, than assistance that you can see. There is always supernatural supply unseen than natural supply that can be seen. I tell you this day says the LORD, as a supernatural woman, you need to operate in SUPERNATURAL EXTREME FAITH in this season, where radical faith and favor in the spirit will manifest your request.

This story offers a rare glimpse of the "invisible world" of supernatural assistance. God has resources to help us that we cannot see. The account picks up in *2 Kings 6:15-18*. *"When the servant of the man of God got up and went out early the next morning, an army with horses and chariots had surrounded the city. 'Oh, my lord, what shall we do?' the servant asked. 'Don't be afraid,' the prophet answered. 'Those who are with us are more than those who are with them.' And Elisha prayed, 'O LORD, open his eyes so he may see.' Then the LORD opened the servant's eyes, and he looked and saw the hills full of horses and chariots of fire all around Elisha. As the enemy came down toward him, Elisha prayed to the LORD, 'Strike these people with blindness.' So he struck them with blindness, as Elisha had asked."*

SUPERNATURAL EXTREME FAITH calls for extreme responses. I tell you this day says the

I'm a supernatural woman, serving a supernatural GOD and getting supernatural results!

LORD, SUPERNATURAL EXTREME FAITH is the answer for "What shall we do?" I tell you don't be afraid. Those who are with us are more than those who are with them." There is an extreme response to your present situation. Do not fear. The supernatural angelic assistance that GOD assigned to HIS righteous remnant is invisible to everyone else, but far outnumbers their enemies.

Supernatural Extreme faith can never be measured with the natural eye. The natural eye only has the capacity to see what already exist. There is an unseen realm of SUPERNATURAL abundance and assistance, whereby every aspect of your life relative to divine protection and divine release is already made available to you, says the LORD. SUPERNATURAL EXTREME FAITH has the power to launch you in to the realm of the impossible. It's that place where your faith supernaturally launches, bypassing demonic realms of unbelief that offer you a challenge along the way but do not have the power to stop your SUPERNATURAL EXTREME FAITH unless you let it.

Supernatural Tips for the Supernatural Woman

SUPERNATURAL EXTREME FAITH is a position in the realm of the spirit where audacity meets expectation by faith and what you believe for comes into manifestation. The tenacity of your faith coupled with the audacity to believe, brings to pass what you ask for in HIS name.

I'm a supernatural woman, serving a supernatural GOD and getting supernatural results!

SUPERNATURAL EXTREME FAITH defies natural reason and supersedes natural comprehension. When I tell you to have faith, says the LORD, I'M not asking you to understand; I'M telling MY righteous remnant to meet ME on MY terms. I tell you says the LORD, I'M not interested in your thoughts, I'M commanding you to tap into MY thoughts and MY ways, it's where SUPERNATURAL EXTREME FAITH awaits you.

MY HOLY SCRIPTURES testify in *Isaiah 55:8-9: "For my thoughts are not your thoughts, neither are your ways my ways," declares the LORD. "As the heavens are higher than the earth, so are my ways higher than your ways and my thoughts than your thoughts.* This day says the LORD; I'M supernaturally inviting MY righteous remnant into MY thoughts and MY ways. SUPERNATURAL EXTREME FAITH is that place where you will witness the SUPERNATURAL EXTREME of MY creation and what's already prepared for everything that I created says the LORD.

Supernatural Tips for the Supernatural Woman

The LORD'S thoughts are full of purpose and destiny. Everything that HE'S already done, including the wisdom behind the purpose of what HE'S already done, HE makes available to the supernatural woman. That wisdom is SUPERNATURALLY EXTREME, says the LORD, and how you obtain by faith what I'VE already done will manifest as EXTREME

I'm a supernatural woman, serving a supernatural GOD and getting supernatural results!

SUPERNATURAL miraculous experiences in your life as a supernatural woman.

When I tell you to come up higher than the realm of the liar, I'M telling you to come into a undisturbed SUPERNATURAL EXTREME place of MY rest where EXTREME resources are available to you. MY thoughts are not your thoughts and MY ways are not your ways, but SUPERNATURAL EXTREME faith is where I'LL reveal what's for you, in the days ahead says the LORD. It's where your believing has broken through the barriers of unbelief. When you supernaturally break through barriers of unbelief, this means that you never forget what I'VE supernaturally already done for you. It's that place where you keep on believing to see what I'M going to do in your present situation. This is where there is no breakdown between believing ME for what already happened and what's to come. When you break through barriers of unbelief, it's because you have positioned yourself in ME, says the LORD, whereby our oneness is never violated. When our supernatural oneness is violated, SUPERNATURAL EXTREME faith is broken.

The lack of repentance nullifies our faith. It puts our faith on hold. SUPERNATURAL EXTREME FAITH is where the pure, holy, and creative power of GOD is available to us, but the lack of repentance is where the devil has fooled us by his schemes and we think that we don't have to do it GOD'S way to get what GOD has. It is where we become justified in demonic injustice.

Supernatural Tips for the Supernatural Woman

Don't break faith with GOD. In the realm of SUPERNATURAL EXTREME faith, Satan is locked out of that realm. The devil can't interrupt what's been designated for your cup, unless you let him.

When we break through barriers of unbelief, it's because we have positioned ourselves in CHRIST where our oneness is never violated. When our reality, relative to doing things in our own strength submits to CHRIST'S supernatural reality, we will say like the Apostle Paul, *I can do all things through Christ who strengthens me*. Then the SUPERNATURAL EXTREME of what I'VE already done for you, says the LORD, will be available to you.

MY HOLY SCRIPTURES testify that the Apostle Paul said in *Philippians 4:13:* "*I can do everything through him who gives me strength.*" The Apostle Paul had a SUPERNATURAL SECRET. He had been shipwrecked, beaten, and imprisoned; Paul had seen the down side of life. He had also known prosperity. But Paul had discovered a secret for contentment in all situations: his deeply personal sense of living in Christ. In this he found strength to handle anything. The Apostle Paul's SUPERNATURAL SECRET was that when he pleased GOD in everything, GOD gave him strength to do everything in Christ. Union with the TRUE and LIVING GOD, is the secret of being content and the source of Paul's abiding extreme faith an strength.

In the SUPERNATURAL EXTREME, super-natural strength is made available to you says the

LORD. The supernatural strength that I had before the foundations of the world and designated for the immediacy of your present situation is supernaturally released and the results are SUPERNATURALLY EXTREME. In SUPERNATURAL EXTREME FAITH, says the LORD, you don't chat with devil. In the SUPERNATURAL EXTREME, you override demonic schemes. Your SUPERNATURAL union with ME, says the LORD shuts his demonic activity down. I, the TRUE and LIVING GOD, AM calling MY righteous remnant to master resisting that devil.

MY HOLY SCRIPTURES testify in *James 4:4:* *"You adulterous people, don't you know that friendship with the world is hatred toward God? Anyone who chooses to be a friend of the world becomes an enemy of God."* The LORD is saying to HIS righteous remnant that there is a level of resisting the devil where HE causes a supernatural separation of friendships that don't benefit your next level of faith and purpose. We could be best friends, but one of us is not GOD's friend. Based on how we master resisting the devil thereby are we promoted in the KINGDOM of GOD. Some who we call friends can't go all the way with us because their level of commitment to GOD is lesser; therefore, they can't access the blessings that GOD has for us.

James 4:5 says, *"Or do you think Scripture says without reason that the spirit he caused to live in us envies intensely?"* The LORD is reminding us in the Book of Genesis after Eve accused the serpent of deceiving her instead of saying that she allowed herself to be deceived by the serpent, GOD said to

I'm a supernatural woman, serving a supernatural GOD and getting supernatural results!

the serpent in ***Genesis 3:5,*** *"And I will put enmity between you and the woman, and between your off-spring and hers; he will crush your head and you will strike his heel."*

The intense struggle between God and the evil one played out in hearts and history of mankind. The offspring of the woman would eventually crush the serpent's head, a promise fulfilled in Christ's victory over Satan, a victory in which all believers share by choice. I tell you this day, says the TRUE and LIVING GOD, master resisting the devil and you will master living in SUPERNATURAL EXTREME FAITH as a supernatural woman.

James 4:6–8: *But he gives us more grace. That is why Scripture says: "God opposes the proud but gives grace to the humble." "Submit yourselves, then, to God. Resist the devil, and he will flee from you. Come near to God and he will come near to you. Wash your hands, you sinners, and purify your hearts, you double-minded."* Let me tell you something: when GOD opposes you, the devil has easy access to you. Humility grants us grace to be in HIS presence. The LORD is saying to us if you submit first to GOD, then you can resist the devil. Supernatural extreme faith does not say "excuse me" to what it's about to invade. Supernatural extreme faith manifests the preordained purposes of GOD whereby what was preordained to be, must exist. Supernatural extreme faith is for the supernatural woman.

Chapter 5

SUPERNATURAL SHEEP THAT THE WOLF CAN'T KEEP

Matthew 10:16.
I am sending you out like sheep among wolves. Therefore be as shrewd as snakes and as innocent as doves.

The Prophetic-Poetic Word
I send you out as sheep among wolves;
this was MY plan of action, says the LORD, before the world's foundations.
I could foresee those who would really follow ME, they dare to operate in the fullness of CHRIST with power and demonstration.

It's their union with ME, says the LORD that allows them to be free.
It's where the wolf's awareness of WHO I AM is hidden and the wolf can't see.

I'm a supernatural woman, serving a supernatural GOD and getting supernatural results!

Salvation's plan was not established after Satan's fall;
it was MY supernatural hidden agenda, says the LORD,
that concealed MY assignment and call.

The all-knowing Father preordained what could not
be prevented.
This is why we can't add or take away from the Holy
Book what's already been prophesied and printed.

I send you out as sheep among wolves where supernatural power already exists.
Be wiser than the serpent and harmless as a dove;
your victories are like a hand that fits in a glove

I tell you this day, says the LORD, the wolf has
already been slain,
and the reverse to every curse already exists.
Supernatural adjustments have already been made for
your comeback after every attack
with an overcoming power to keep the wolf off the
sheep's back.

Supernatural Sheep that the Wolf Can't Keep

The LORD has supernaturally enhance the reality of HIS righteous remnant and granted them the capacity, relative to HIS HOLY SCRIPTURES, to understand the original intent as to why HE sent them out as sheep among wolves. The first thing that the LORD wants us to understand is that the wolf is part of HIS creation and HIS creation will never rule over HIM. To every intent and purpose, says the LORD of MY creation, I hold the explicit accuracy as to how everything functions that I created and what it will do. I, the TRUE and LIVING GOD have already positioned MY righteous remnant to rule with ME. As MY righteous remnant chooses to rule with ME, nothing will overcome them. Therefore, says the LORD, MY righteous remnant hold that same capacity and fullness of MY supernatural power to rule over the wolf.

I'M calling every supernatural woman to a holy alertness in this hour so that deviation or heresy won't cripple their access to operate in MY fullness. This is the hour to walk in MY completeness, says the LORD. It's a supernatural place of wisdom and power to defeat the wolf in this hour.

Supernatural Tips for the Supernatural Woman

You can be smart or super-intelligent but the wolf still has access to you when your mind is not submitted to CHRIST. I, the TRUE and LIVING GOD,

I'm a supernatural woman, serving a supernatural GOD and getting supernatural results!

have already positioned MY righteous remnant to rule with ME.

The Apostle Paul confirms and asserts that true fullness is found only in Christ. The account picks up where the HOLY SCRIPTURES testify in *Colossians 2:9-15*: *"For in Christ all the fullness of the Deity lives in bodily form, and you have been given fullness in Christ, who is the head over every power and authority. In him you were also circumcised, in the putting off of the sinful nature, not with a circumcision done by the hands of men but with the circumcision done by Christ, having been buried with him in baptism and raised with him through your faith in the power of God, who raised him from the dead. When you were dead in your sins and in the un-circumcision of your sinful nature, God made you alive with Christ. He forgave us all our sins, having canceled the written code, with its regulations, that was against us and that stood opposed to us; he took it away, nailing it to the cross. And having disarmed the powers and authorities, he made a public spectacle of them, triumphing over them by the cross."*

I tell you this day, says the LORD, I'M calling you to operate in MY fullness. The wolf has already been slain and the reverse to every curse already exist. Supernatural adjustments have already been made for your comeback after every attack with an overcoming power to keep the wolf off the sheep's back. Let this become your supernatural reality and confession... *I am a supernatural sheep that the wolf can't keep.*

What I rule over, says the LORD, was never designed with the capacity or power to rule over ME.

I'm a supernatural woman, serving a supernatural GOD and getting supernatural results!

When MY righteous remnant rule with ME, says the LORD, MY creation is subject to them. Before the foundations of the world MY original intent for MY righteous remnant, was to operate and function in holy supernatural capacities whereby victorious daily outcomes in their lives would be a direct result of what I'VE already accomplished for their lives.

On the sixth day of MY creation, prior to MY creating ADAM and EVE, it was already in the mind of GOD to establish equal ruling privileges for man. MY HOLY SCRIPTURES testify in **Genesis 1:26-27:** *"Then God said, "Let us make man in our image, in our likeness, and let them rule over the fish of the sea and the birds of the air, over the livestock, over all the earth, and over all the creatures that move along the ground." So God created man in his own image, in the image of God he created him; male and female he created them."*

I tell you again this day, says the LORD, what I rule over was never designed with the capacity or power to rule over ME. When MY righteous remnant rule with ME, says the LORD, MY creation is subject to them. They are victorious sheep in a world of wolves. Let this become your supernatural reality and confession: *I am a supernatural sheep that the wolf can't keep*. Let's get one supernatural thing straight, says the LORD, do you think that the all-knowing, all-seeing and all-understanding GOD would send HIS sheep out among wolves, if they were not already granted the supernatural capacity and power to maintain a position of victory in ME, says the LORD, where the wolf was already defeated?

I'm a supernatural woman, serving a supernatural GOD and getting supernatural results!

I'M not asking you to go out and defeat a wolf; I'M telling you to supernaturally operate in a realm where I'VE already defeated that wolf. MY supernatural objective in this hour, says the LORD, is to get you as a supernatural woman to see that living in ME is where you need to be. When you lag outside of the SHEPHERD'S boundaries says the LORD, you are open game for the wolf. There are supernatural victorious behavior patterns only in ME, says the LORD that positions MY righteous remnant to automatically escape the wolf's grip. If I'M not on automatic pilot in you in this hour, the wolf will devour you. Let this become your supernatural reality and confession. *I am a supernatural sheep that the wolf can't keep.*

MY HOLY SCRIPTURES testify in **Matthew 10:16**. *I am sending you out like sheep among wolves. Therefore be as shrewd as snakes and as innocent as doves*. The LORD is saying, "I want you to be wise about what is good, and innocent about what is evil." When I tell you to be shrewd as a snake, I'M telling you to use MY pure wisdom, which has supernatural insightful holy perspectives and which are downloaded in the very moment that you need them. I, the TRUE and LIVING GOD will keep you supernaturally alert in the presence of wolves.

Supernatural Tips for the Supernatural Woman

Wolves are after your flesh and appeal to your appetite whether spiritual or natural. They can only lure you with what's already in you: that which is not

I'm a supernatural woman, serving a supernatural GOD and getting supernatural results!

dead in CHRIST. Snakes are low-level wolves that manifest their agenda over those who don't surrender.

To be "innocent as a dove" means to be guided by the pureness of MY HOLY SPIRIT in the presence of wolves. Keep your hands clean; be innocent when it comes to evil activity. When you purpose to live a holy and blameless life, you will see the wolf, but the wolf can't see you. Holiness is the light that I AM says the LORD. When you live holy as I AM holy, says the LORD, you will see the dark activities that the wolf is trying to implement as he attempts to devour your light.

MY HOLY SCRIPTURES testify in *1Peter 1:15-16*: *"But just as he who called you is holy, so be holy in all you do; for it is written: "Be holy, because I am holy."* To be holy is to be set apart, set apart from sin and impurity, and set apart unto God. This is the complete moral perfection of God, whose eyes are too pure to look on evil with favor. The LORD is saying to HIS supernatural women, "I want you to be wise about what is good, and innocent about what is evil. Don't look on evil with favor, that's the behavior pattern of a wolf."

Supernatural Tips for the Supernatural Woman

It's your union with ME, says the LORD that allows you to be free. It's where the wolf's awareness of WHO I AM is hidden in you and he can't see. Stop losing your identity in the wilderness of life's storms. Trust ME when you can't trace ME. The wolf doesn't know how I'M going to deliver you. As a supernatural woman you are already equipped not to slip.

MY HOLY SCRIPTURES testify in **Matthew 7** of how I warned the people and told them how to recognize a wolf. They are people who claim to have been sent by GOD but they are not. They sound like it, but there is no indication based on their life-styles that they live by the Word of GOD or that GOD is living in them. They read books and even preach while claiming another man's revelation without being processed by the words they read.

BE ALERT, says the LORD...I can open your eyes to another man's revelation if I deem you ready to live in that revelation, but you will not and can't obtain the experience behind that revelation unless you've obeyed ME through the experience of that situation. That's why people will say, "If I were you, I wouldn't take that or I don't know how you do it. You must be crazy to go through all of that, or it don't take all that." As a supernatural woman you can say, "You need to shut up until you live in my shoes." If you ask GOD to open your eyes, you'll see that the wolf is not devouring me, he's still devouring you, because you aren't ready to give up what the LORD is asking you to die to."

The wolf can look the part and sound the part, but he is not part of MY flock says the LORD. The account picks up in *Matthew 7:15-20: "Watch out for false prophets. They come to you in sheep's clothing, but inwardly they are ferocious wolves. By their fruit you will recognize them. Do people pick grapes from thorn bushes, or figs from thistles? Likewise every*

I'm a supernatural woman, serving a supernatural GOD and getting supernatural results!

good tree bears good fruit, but a bad tree bears bad fruit. A good tree cannot bear bad fruit, and a bad tree cannot bear good fruit. Every tree that does not bear good fruit is cut down and thrown into the fire. Thus, by their fruit you will recognize them."

The wolf can look like sheep. They sound like sheep, but they are not sheep and they are wolves in sheep's clothing. They are disruptive, unruly, and fierce; they look on evil with favor, taking in evil reports with ease, but they are not MY sheep, says the LORD.

I knew about that wolf before I created HIM, says the LORD, and what purpose I'D use him for. MY HOLY SCRIPTURES testify in *Isaiah 54:16-17:* *"See, it is I who created the blacksmith who fans the coals into flame and forges a weapon fit for its work. And it is I who have created the destroyer to work havoc; no weapon forged against you will prevail, and you will refute every tongue that accuses you. This is the heritage of the servants of the LORD, and this is their vindication from me," declares the LORD.*

The one who was created can never overpower the one who created him. I created that devil with the supernatural intent of MY righteous remnant to defeat him. There is a supernatural resistance that MY righteous remnants possess through MY HOLY WORD that the wolf can't overpower. I tell you this day says the LORD, be still and master the freedom of a surrendered will. Stop asking yourselves why GOD would create a devil. You need to position yourselves in CHRIST to overcome that devil. I'VE already scheduled your blessings and promises based

I'm a supernatural woman, serving a supernatural GOD and getting supernatural results!

on MY supernatural hidden agenda that the wolf is not aware of says the LORD.

I already know your temptations and I'VE already positioned supernatural outcomes of goodness and mercy that follow surrendered wills. You are only safe from the wolf if your will is surrendered to ME, says the LORD. Remember, I'M not asking you to go out and defeat a wolf; I'M telling you to supernaturally operate in a realm where I'VE already defeated that wolf. MY supernatural objective in this hour, says the LORD, is to get you to see that living in ME is where you need to be. Let this become your supernatural reality and confession: *I am a supernatural sheep that the wolf can't keep*.

Supernatural Tips for the Supernatural Woman

Supernatural adjustments have already been made for your comeback after every attack with an overcoming power to keep the wolf off the sheep's back. Cast your care and don't walk in fear.

Chapter 6

THE SUPERNATURAL MOMENTUM OF THE LORD

Psalm 18:33
He makes my feet like the feet of a deer; he causes me to stand on the heights.

The Prophetic-Poetic Word

Forge Ahead!
March forward and step high,
for I have given unto you hinds feet for high places.
The territory that I have given you, says the Lord,
is territory already supernaturally taken.
I've unlocked doors for the Body of Christ,
and the doors that I shut the enemy can't break in.

There is an open window whereby time created by
ME, says the LORD, must be respected.
Don't be fooled by manifested destruction;

I'm a supernatural woman, serving a supernatural GOD and getting supernatural results!

move forward the righteous are supernaturally
protected.

Your armor must be in place says the LORD,
it's where the enemy can't see your face.
My shield of faith has a blinding effect;
gifts and spoils have already been taken and given to
the select.
My inheritance has a designated distribution,
for the time has come for full restitution.

The Supernatural Momentum of the Lord

The SPIRIT OF THE LIVING GOD is saying to HIS supernatural woman, "I'M supernaturally in charge and reign sovereignly over everything and everyone. When I tell you to move forward and step high, it's because I have already mastered your rough terrain. I'VE already scouted out the land on your behalf.

When you step high, this means that you will march in MY confidence. This means that what I say or every command that I give has already been preloaded with whatever you need to carry it out. I will never tell you to forge ahead without having already prepared you for what I'M giving you access to, says the LORD.

Don't operate in doubt like that devil, says the LORD. When he was trying to tempt ME, in the wilderness, he had me standing on the highest point in the temple and said "if you are the Son of GOD." That devil was trying to test ME, the TRUE and LIVING GOD with scriptures that I had already written before the foundation of the world. What was preordained before the foundations of the world had not yet manifested relative to WHO I AM, says the LORD.

The HOLY SCRIPTURES testify in *Matthew 4:5-7: "Then the devil took him to the holy city and had him stand on the highest point of the temple. "If you are the Son of God," he said, "throw yourself down. For it is written: "He will command his angels concerning you, and they will lift you up in their hands, so that you will not strike your foot against a*

I'm a supernatural woman, serving a supernatural GOD and getting supernatural results!

62

stone. Jesus answered him, "It is also written: 'Do not put the Lord your God to the test."

Supernatural Tips for the Supernatural Woman

The temptations in life always come to test you, but when the ME in you, WHO IS THE CHRIST in you responds to the temptation or the test, you won't bow to the tempter either. You will be able to stand on what's already written. This is what will cause you to forge ahead in the days ahead. When I tell you says the LORD, I'VE already conquered your rough terrain, I'M telling you that the oneness of WHO I AM relative to MY HOLY WORD, was already written in the midst of the devil trying to test ME. This could never be altered because it's impossible for the tempter to tamper with his Creator.

It is written in ***Proverbs 24:16:*** *"for though the righteous fall seven times, they rise again, but the wicked stumble when calamity strikes."* Get up, says the LORD, The territory that I have given you is territory already supernaturally taken. I've unlocked doors for the Body of Christ, and the doors that I shut the enemy can't break in. Get up and forge ahead. I have already prepared the way for you, says the LORD. Trust ME and supernaturally take a step.

I'VE given you hind's feet in high places. The HOLY SCRIPTURES testify in ***Psalm 18:32-34:*** *"It is God who arms me with strength and keeps my way secure. He makes my feet like the feet of a deer; he causes me to stand on the heights. He trains my hands for battle; my arms can bend a bow of bronze."* The

I'm a supernatural woman, serving a supernatural GOD and getting supernatural results!

LORD is saying I'VE armed you with MY strength; your security is in ME. I'M calling you to walk where I'VE already walked. It's not like I'M sending you into strange places, I already walked on and subdued every high place. I'VE trained your hands for battle by taking the battle out of your hands so that you reap from the victory that I'VE already won. This is supernaturally so, says the SPIRIT OF THE LIVING GOD.

I tell you this day says the LORD, I'VE carved an opening in time through opening heaven's window. Don't be dismayed for the LORD thy GOD is with thee. Forge ahead. Don't be entangled with the signs of the times or be overwhelmed with them. It is written, this is what's to come. What's happening in time must answer to my sovereignty. MY righteous indignation has already intervened, and justified judgments have already been supernaturally activated, says the LORD.

Nothing can stop a sovereign process. What I have already put in place, says the LORD, cannot be replaced. What I bless no man can curse. What I curse no man can lift. What I'VE preordained to supernaturally be imparted into the lives of the righteous, everything that is not supposed to be there when I'M ready to supernaturally impart the blessing must leave. Forge ahead says the LORD the opening is here, doors, windows, opportunities coupled with MY favor are currently in high activation says the LORD. Let the dogs bark; let the dogs bark and forge ahead!

The HOLY SCRIPTURES testify in ***Philippians 3:1-3***: *"Further, my brothers and sisters, rejoice in the*

I'm a supernatural woman, serving a supernatural GOD and getting supernatural results!

Lord! It is no trouble for me to write the same things to you again, and it is a safeguard for you. Watch out for those dogs, those evildoers, those mutilators of the flesh. For it is we who are the circumcision, we who serve God by his Spirit, who boast in Christ Jesus, and who put no confidence in the flesh." The supernatural woman serves GOD in the spirit, and is led by HIS HOLY SPIRIT. She makes her boast in the LORD. She has the confidence of GOD, even if she hears the dogs barking she is not moved. Let the dogs bark; let the dogs bark … Forge ahead, says the SPIRIT OF THE LIVING GOD. Don't be fooled by manifested destruction; move forward. I will supernaturally protect the righteous, says the LORD. Your armor must be in place; it's where the enemy can't see your face.

I tell you this day, says the TRUE AND LIVING GOD, MY shield of faith is supernaturally blinding to the enemy. A measure of faith was never given to the devil, and he is not privy to this supernatural communication level in the spirit between GOD and HIS people. This is why his objective is to steal, kill, and destroy. It serves as a distraction to attack your faith.

The HOLY SCRIPTURES testify in *Ephesians 6:10-16:* "*In addition to all this, take up the shield of faith, with which you can extinguish all the flaming arrows of the evil one.*" The shield of faith that blinds the enemy is that supernatural light that reflects from the life of the believer in the spirit, when they are aligned with CHRIST. It's able to extinguish, quench, and snuff out every flaming arrow from the enemy's camp.

I'm a supernatural woman, serving a supernatural GOD and getting supernatural results!

65

Finally, it is crucial to recognize the supernatural momentum of the SPIRIT OF THE LORD. It's riding on the prophetic revelation of a now word. Opposition can't stand against GOD's supernatural transition; HE comes to place you in a new position.

Chapter 7

SUPERNATURAL LIVING IS HOLY GHOST DRIVEN

John 16:13–14
Howbeit when he, the Spirit of truth, is come,
he will guide you into all truth: for he shall not
speak of himself; but whatsoever he shall hear,
that shall he speak: and he will show you things
to come. [14]He shall glorify me: for he shall
receive of mine, and shall show it unto you.

The Prophetic-Poetic Word
I say to MY righteous remnant that I have a designer
lifestyle,
for those who are bold enough to live through ME.
It's supernatural living that's HOLY GHOST- driven,
whereby those who are led by faith can see.

This lifestyle is designed to live under an open heaven

I'm a supernatural woman, serving a supernatural GOD and getting supernatural results!

with supernatural access to holy dialogue and direction.
It's where you rise above confusion, live in the moment,
under supernatural divine protection.

This designer lifestyle has GOD's seal of approval.
It shows up as a mark in the forehead of the chosen and the few
whose supernatural blueprint was preordained to roll out on cue.

It's a realm where natural impossibilities are supernaturally possible.
It's where the overshadowing of GOD'S existence has tangible effects.
It's a place where Kingdom treasure is dispensed to those who GOD selects.

It's where immediate obedience stands ready to heed Holy Spirit's unction.
Supernatural living unfolds the victory that's stored up for the righteous to function.
Never underestimate the power of HOLY GHOST-driven, supernatural living,
it's time to unfold what's been foretold about receiving and giving.

I'm a supernatural woman, serving a supernatural GOD and getting supernatural results!

Supernatural Living HOLY GHOST Driven

There is a no-nonsense realm in the supernatural that is holy and sanctified unto ME, says the LORD. It's a place where I'VE drawn the boundary lines whereby sin can't get in. In the days ahead, mastering being led by MY HOLY SPIRIT is where supernatural living for the supernatural woman exists. It's that place of knowing in advance that sin is always crouched down at your door, waiting for an opportunity to get in. The lifestyle that I'M calling MY righteous remnant to live in operates from eternity, although its activity can be carried out within time. It's a timeless place with supernatural results.

The HOLY SCRIPTURES testify in **Genesis, Chapter 4** of how I reminded Cain that sin is crouched down at the door, just as sin is waiting at your door, seeking to get in where it's never been before in time. The account picks up in ***Genesis 4:2-7***: *"And Adam knew Eve his wife; and she conceived, and bare Cain, and said, I have gotten a man from the LORD. And she again bare his brother Abel. And Abel was a keeper of sheep, but Cain was a tiller of the ground. And in process of time it came to pass, that Cain brought of the fruit of the ground an offering unto the LORD. And Abel, he also brought of the firstlings of his flock and of the fat thereof. And the LORD had respect unto Abel and to his offering: But unto Cain and to his offering he had not respect. And Cain was very wroth, and his countenance fell. And the LORD said unto Cain, Why art thou wroth? and why is thy countenance fallen? [7]If thou doest well, shall thou not*

I'm a supernatural woman, serving a supernatural GOD and getting supernatural results!

be accepted? and if thou doest not well, sin lieth at the door. And unto thee shall be his desire, and thou shall rule over him."

Please note that in the process of time, as a supernatural woman, you must be processed by ME within time, says the LORD. It's possible to know of ME and not let ME, the TRUE and LIVING GOD, process you. You must be careful, says the LORD, to allow ME to process you so that I will be pleased with your offerings, even your sacrifice of praise. If it's not done on MY terms, I won't be pleased with you, says the LORD. Although I'M no respecter of persons and whosoever will, may come, this means that I'M giving everyone a chance to do it on MY terms, says the LORD. Unless I process you, within the process of time, you won't be prepared to give ME what I'M looking for from you, says the LORD

Because Cain lacked the willingness to be processed by ME, he never positioned his heart to be pleasing to ME. Therefore he could not give ME his best, says the LORD. How can you offer ME your best when you refuse to yield to MY terms? I never had Cain's heart, says the LORD, and I still gave him the opportunity to repent and do the righteous thing. Whenever an offering is brought before ME, MY desire is that it be your first and your best, says the LORD. Please notice that I came to Cain before sin leaped on him. Sin is a satanic spirit that watches everyone in the earth realm; its opening is disobedience. This spirit is able to override a un-submitted or un-surrendered will at any time, thereby overruling the will of those who refuse to submit to the will of GOD.

I'm a supernatural woman, serving a supernatural GOD and getting supernatural results!

Supernatural Tips for the Supernatural Woman

In the supernatural living, HOLY GHOST- driven life, don't allow sin to override your will or it will overrule you. I, the TRUE and LIVING GOD over- came so that MY righteous remnant can OVERCOME.

The supernatural living, HOLY GHOST- driven life, is a sin-free life, designed and pre-ordained before time to be manifested through our LORD and Savior Jesus Christ. HE became our living example. JESUS, taking His instructions from His Father, walking out what was preordained and written, followed holy instructions that supernaturally empowered Christians to overcome. HE came down to the level of sinful man, overcame man's sinful nature, and established supernatural behavior patterns in order to outwit sin. From His birth through His resurrection, everything that He said and did was supernatural. It is crucial that the mind of CHRIST is operating through us in order to access this supernatural lifestyle.

The HOLY SCRIPTURES testify how the Apostle Paul described the supernatural lifestyle of Jesus in *Philippians 4:1-11:* *"If there be therefore any conso- lation in Christ, if any comfort of love, if any fellow- ship of the Spirit, if any bowels and mercies, Fulfill ye my joy, that ye be likeminded, having the same love, being of one accord, of one mind. Let nothing be done through strife or vainglory; but in lowliness of mind let each esteem other better than themselves. Look not every man on his own things, but every man also on the things of others. Let this mind be in you, which was also in Christ Jesus: Who, being in the*

I'm a supernatural woman, serving a supernatural GOD and getting supernatural results!

form of God, thought it not robbery to be equal with God: But made himself of no reputation, and took upon him the form of a servant, and was made in the likeness of men: And being found in fashion as a man, he humbled himself, and became obedient unto death, even the death of the cross. Wherefore God also hath highly exalted him, and given him a name which is above every name: That at the name of Jesus every knee should bow, of things in heaven, and things in earth, and things under the earth; And that every tongue should confess that Jesus Christ is Lord, to the glory of God the Father."

The Supernatural living, HOLY GHOST-driven lifestyle has access to supernatural holy dialogue through the mind of CHRIST, as the righteous are led. This dialogue or communication is holy foreknowledge for our present situation. Because CHRIST was obedient unto death, there is no situation that the righteous exist in that the answer or way of escape is not already available. When we are led by the HOLY SPIRIT, we are supernaturally engaged with the wisdom, knowledge and understanding of GOD, HIMSELF, whereby, we walk out what has already been written about our lives.

The Holy Scriptures testify in *John 16:13-14:* *"Howbeit when he, the Spirit of truth, is come, he will guide you into all truth: for he shall not speak of himself; but whatsoever he shall hear, that shall he speak: and he will show you things to come. He shall glorify me: for he shall receive of mine, and shall show it unto you."* The supernatural living, HOLY GHOST-driven lifestyle positions the righteous to

I'm a supernatural woman, serving a supernatural GOD and getting supernatural results!

supernaturally interact with the HOLY SPIRIT. The HOLY SPIRIT will speak, but not speak of HIMSELF. HE will speak what HE hears, so the HOLY SPIRIT will hear from JESUS and tell us what JESUS is saying. The supernatural conversation that FATHER, SON, and HOLY SPIRIT had before the foundations of the world is downloaded into the righteous. JESUS is communicating with the HOLY SPIRIT, and the HOLY SPIRIT is communicating with the righteous of how the victory was already won. Supernatural dialogue for the supernatural living, HOLY GHOST-driven lifestyle is a constant download of revelation, wisdom, knowledge, and understanding.

Supernatural Tips for the Supernatural Woman

The supernatural dialogue with the HOLY GHOST is where I'm driven for supernatural living. It's where we overcome the outcome.

I'm a supernatural woman, serving a supernatural GOD and getting supernatural results!

Chapter 8

THE SUPERNATURAL FORCE OF RIGHTEOUSNESS

The Prophetic-Poetic Word

There is a supernatural momentum in righteousness driven by truth,
whereby it's course never goes off track.
There is an overriding force prevailing for the righteous,
it's wherever truth is spoken it can't be taken back.

Righteousness dares to tread on unfamiliar ground,
it has an indignation that makes anything unstable sound.
The rules of righteousness were established in holiness,
it's where no room for sin can be found.
The pathway of the righteous is always bright,
no attack from the enemy's camp can keep the righteous bound.

The momentum within righteousness will thrust forth no matter how dark the scheme,
it's where Satan himself was shocked by the resurrection of Jesus Christ.
The surmounting triumphant overcoming power of the righteous,
can never be stopped because it's backed up by God's supernaturally paid price.

Righteousness is a force that can't be reckoned with,
it is the very characteristic of the Holy Trinity's persona.
The supernatural momentum of righteousness has a force,
it's where there is a continuous release of power, authority, and honor.

The Supernatural Force of Righteousness

The LORD is declaring to HIS supernatural women that there is a constant supernatural momentum for those who operate within the force of righteousness. It surmounts, overcomes and prevails because it is driven by the SPIRIT OF TRUTH. The HOLY SCRIPTURES reveals to us that truth describes and identifies who JESUS CHRIST is. The **Gospel of John** reveals to us a conversation that JESUS was having with HIS disciples, about the rooms in HIS FATHER'S house, coupled with a place HE was going to prepare for them and that HE was coming back for them. This didn't sit right with one of the LORD'S disciples, called Thomas, who didn't understand. So JESUS told him how HE, JESUS, could be identified. In *John 14:5-6, Thomas said to him, "Lord, we don't know where you are going, so how can we know the way?" Jesus answered, "I am the way and the truth and the life. No one comes to the Father except through me."* JESUS was telling him, after I leave, don't follow anyone but ME and MY teachings. You will be able to identify with the truth of WHO I AM, for the Word of GOD is true and I AM one with MY Word. Furthermore, no one can be saved, come to salvation, or comprehend WHO I AM or know the real truth, unless they come through ME, says the LORD. If they don't come through ME, they will not be received by MY FATHER.

Supernatural Tips for the Supernatural Woman

Being identified with CHRIST is where we have access to HIS knowledge, wisdom and decrement. "Doubting Thomas days" are over for the supernatural woman. As righteous supernatural women, we are a force to be reckoned with.

The "supernatural force within righteousness" establishes the newness of life in the earth realm, whereby every step taken in righteousness is a step that increases with fruitfulness and power. The HOLY SCRIPTURES reveal to us the Apostle Paul's instruction to the Philippians, relative to the progress of their momentum. ***Philippians 1:9-11*** *"And this is my prayer: that your love may abound more and more in knowledge and depth of insight, so that you may be able to discern what is best and may be pure and blameless until the day of Christ, filled with the fruit of righteousness that comes through Jesus Christ to the glory and praise of God."* The Apostle Paul identifies that only through Jesus Christ, can we be filled with the fruit of righteousness. It has an abundant growing momentum through love that increases our knowledge and insight enabling us to discern the best, by living pure lives until the day of CHRIST. This is where the supernatural force of righteousness maintains its momentum in our lives. Remember as righteous supernatural women, we are a force to be reckoned with.

The supernatural force of righteousness has power to change things. There are unseen forces that cringe and flee because of the supernatural force of

I'm a supernatural woman, serving a supernatural GOD and getting supernatural results!

righteousness. It destroys any hint of darkness lurking in its path. The supernatural force of righteousness lays its own tracks. It's like Mack Trucks in some of the worst weather conditions, which leave deeply embedded tracks after its tires roll over snow-covered roads. That's where smaller cars and trucks can follow with ease.

Just as the supernatural woman walks in righteousness, she leaves examples, or tracks, of pre-established righteousness, whereby others can follow. After all, the righteous walk in what CHRIST walked out by the example HE established in the earth realm.

The supernatural force of righteousness is a force established by GOD HIMSELF that prevails over the enemy. It is so powerful, that it overrides, stamps out, and exposes every lie. When the force of righteousness is released in the atmosphere, it establishes new life, expels fear, replaces old behavior patterns, and brings correction to a troubled soul.

The HOLY SCRIPTURES reveal the Word of God spoken by the Prophet Isaiah in *Isaiah 54:14-17:* *"In righteousness you will be established: Tyranny will be far from you; you will have nothing to fear. Terror will be far removed; it will not come near you. If anyone does attack you, it will not be my doing; whoever attacks you will surrender to you. See, it is I who created the blacksmith who fans the coals into flame and forges a weapon fit for its work. And it is I who have created the destroyer to work havoc; no weapon forged against you will prevail, and you will refute every tongue that accuses you. This is the*

I'm a supernatural woman, serving a supernatural GOD and getting supernatural results!

heritage of the servants of the LORD, and this is their vindication from me," declares the LORD."

Righteousness is our inheritance. GOD, WHO created the destroyer to work havoc also has full control of how much havoc the destroyer can work. As we allow ourselves to be established in the righteousness of GOD, by allowing the Word of GOD to correct us, we will walk in holiness and righteousness. It's where we can see the weapon being formed and at the same time know that it can't prosper. This powerful position causes us to prevail over the enemy, while the Word of GOD is working for us. The "surmounting force of righteousness" provides supernatural back up for the supernatural woman. Sometimes we must shut up and hold our peace and let the LORD fight our battle. The HOLY SCRIPTURES testify in ***Psalm 31:1,*** *"In you, O LORD, I have taken refuge; let me never be put to shame; deliver me in your righteousness."* This must become the cry of the supernatural woman. We will take refuge in our GOD, and HE will deliver us in HIS righteousness.

We are in a timeslot where righteous indignation, which is a righteous anger, will rise up in believers who take a stand for righteousness, based on injustices to oneself or others. Sometimes we suffer for righteousness' sake, which means that we will be falsely accused, misunderstood or perceived wrongly for something that we are doing right. This is where we come up against conditions and situations that must be dealt with that require heartfelt emotion, quick and sound decisions, and flexibility, coupled with speaking the truth in love. This is where

I'm a supernatural woman, serving a supernatural GOD and getting supernatural results!

righteous solutions to everyday problems must be addressed before sin has an opportunity to take root. Righteousness indignation is so powerful; it's able to make anything that's unstable sound.

In the process of moving forward in the established rules of righteousness, we must be careful not to sin in the process or we will forfeit the CHRIST life that righteousness already established. The HOLY SCRIPTURES tell us in the book of *James 1:19-21:* *"My dear brothers, take note of this: Everyone should be quick to listen, slow to speak and slow to become angry, for man's anger does not bring about the righteous life that God desires. Therefore, get rid of all moral filth and the evil that is so prevalent and humbly accept the word planted in you, which can save you."*

Supernatural Tips for the Supernatural Woman

Every time the supernatural force of righteousness is in operation, unfamiliar ground is treaded upon. As supernatural women we must be ready to give up the old ground for the new unfamiliar ground. It's where the new life in CHRIST unfolds, based on the preordained, established rules of righteousness. The rules of righteousness were established in holiness; it's where no room for sin can be found.

The HOLY SCRIPTURES testify in *Psalm 5:8:"Lead me, O LORD, in your righteousness because of my enemies...make straight your way before me."* The awesome thing about the supernatural force of righteousness is that it supernaturally

I'm a supernatural woman, serving a supernatural GOD and getting supernatural results!

brightens the pathway of the righteous. This pathway remains bright, exposing all demonic activity that attempts to step into its brightness. As supernatural women we must be aware that Satan is the master deceiver, and his servants masquerade as servants of righteousness. So it's based on the righteousness of GOD actively operating in us, which enables our light to shine brighter than those who masquerade as servants of righteousness.

Supernatural Tips for the Supernatural Woman

Pretense is always the enemy's defense, it's where offense manifest as his nonsense. The righteousness of GOD always exposes the enemy's schemes. Keep walking in the righteousness of GOD so you can see.
MY HOLY SCRIPTURES testify in **2 *Corinthians 11:14-15***: *"And no wonder, for Satan himself masquerades as an angel of light. It is not surprising, then, if his servants masquerade as servants of righteousness." Their end will be what their actions deserve.* Let this be known, says the LORD, that Satan and his deceivers are already factored into MY judgments. It is crucial that true believers are walking in the righteousness of God and not their own. It's where the supernatural force of righteousness has already established a living and eternal light that only shines through CHRIST. It's a place where the righteous have graduated from reacting in their flesh. I tell you this day, says the LORD, negative attractions in the physical realm are manifested demonic actions. I'M saying to MY righteous remnant, see through the

light of the GOSPEL OF JESUS CHRIST, and see it from MY perspective. Manifested demonic actions is where demons look to inhabit human bodies for the purpose of doing their bidding or acting out their demonic plans. Just as in the natural realm the lesser light is swallowed up by the brighter light, so is it in the realm of the spirit. The light of holiness in the righteous shines brighter than any devil.

In our pursuit of righteousness, because it's the righteousness of GOD, we will supernaturally interact with the love of GOD, and because we love GOD we have access to the supernatural life in CHRIST. This positions us and grants us access to supernatural prosperity, where the manifestation of whatever we need appears. It's where the supernatural favor of GOD rest on our lives causing others to honor us. The HOLY SCRIPTURES testify in ***Proverbs 21:21:*** *"He who pursues righteousness and love finds life, prosperity and honor."*

I'm a supernatural woman, serving a supernatural GOD and getting supernatural results!

Chapter 9

HOLY SUPERNATURAL REVELATION EXPOSES ALL IMITATION

Acts 2:16-17

*No, this is what was spoken by the prophet
Joel: "In the last days, God says, I will
pour out my Spirit on all people. Your sons
and daughters will prophesy, your young
men will see visions, your old men will
dream dreams."*

The Prophetic-Poetic Word

It's impossible for holy revelation and sin to blend,
it's like the great gulf; set a fixed place that houses
hell and sin.

The hour has come where distinction has a mighty
voice,
it's that place where I the LORD has already gather
MY chosen.

I'm a supernatural woman, serving a supernatural GOD and getting supernatural results!

Their hearts are separated from sin and fornication
and they can supernaturally discern when the enemy
is attempting to close in.

Holy revelation and sin can never blend,
it's like the anti-Christ attempting to deceive the
very elect.
Imitators are limited to places where they can operate,
their lack of originality exposes them as a reject.

I'M the CHRIST, THE REVELATOR, THE SON OF
THE LIVING GOD,
I witnessed the imitator fall from heaven.
It was pre-ordained before creation,
the bread of life needed no leaven.

This is the hour where blameless victories will manifest through holy strategies,
it's where the imitator is not privy to how I already
brought the righteous through.
Holy revelation exposes all imitation,
its where overcomers overthrow the devil on cue!

Supernatural Holy Revelation Exposes All Imitation

The hour has come where I'M pouring MY SPIRIT out upon all flesh, says the LORD. A HOLY distinction has hit the land; it's that place where holy supernatural revelation is exposing all imitation. What looks clean to you, says the LORD, is not necessarily clean to ME, and unless you are experiencing the supernatural living activity of MY HOLY SPIRIT within you that enables you or permits you to see the imitation of demonic activity, that imitation will become a limitation for you. It's impossible for holy revelation and sin to blend. The hour has come where I'M pouring MY SPIRIT out upon all flesh says the LORD. A HOLY distinction has hit the land.

Supernatural Tips for the Supernatural Woman

Don't let the imitator limit you. What's clean to you may not be clean to GOD.

The HOLY SCRIPTURES testify in *Acts 2,* on the day of Pentecost, in a place where MY disciples were waiting on the promised HOLY SPIRIT, says the LORD, suddenly, like the sound of a violent wind, which symbolizes the audible breath or wind of the SPIRIT of GOD, came from heaven and filled the whole house where they were sitting. The fire of MY HOLY SPIRIT which is MY presence, fell on them separately, says the LORD, and they began to speak in other tongues as the SPIRIT enabled them. Some even thought that they were drunk.

I'm a supernatural woman, serving a supernatural GOD and getting supernatural results!

Their spirits were completely under the control of the MY Spirit; says the LORD; their words were MY words, heaven's language on other tongues. They were able to speak in languages as MY HOLY SPIRIT enabled them: languages which they had not previously learned. I tell you this day, says the LORD, just as the sudden coming of MY HOLY SPIRIT came in on the day of Pentecost, so will it be on the day of MY coming. I will suddenly rush in and gather MY righteous remnant. The only difference is, there will also be real drunk people who really won't know what's going on... until they realize that they have been left behind, says the LORD. I tell you this day that the last days are upon us, says the LORD.

The HOLY SCRIPTURES testify in *Acts 2:14-21:* *"Then Peter stood up with the Eleven, raised his voice and addressed the crowd: "Fellow Jews and all of you who live in Jerusalem, let me explain this to you; listen carefully to what I say. These men are not drunk, as you suppose. It's only nine in the morning! No, this is what was spoken by the prophet Joel: 17 'In the last days, God says, I will pour out my Spirit on all people. Your sons and daughters will prophesy, your young men will see visions, your old men will dream dreams. 18 Even on my servants, both men and women, I will pour out my Spirit in those days, and they will prophesy. 19 I will show wonders in the heaven above and signs on the earth below, blood and fire and billows of smoke. The sun will be turned to darkness and the moon to blood before the coming of the great and glorious day of the Lord. And everyone who calls on the name of the Lord will be saved."*

I'm a supernatural woman, serving a supernatural GOD and getting supernatural results!

The living truth of MY salvation is so powerful that it is able to save those who call on MY NAME. MY HOLY SPIRIT living in MY supernatural women is that supernatural separator from the imitator. MY poured-out Spirit will lead them in the living path of the revelator, says the LORD.

Supernatural Tips for the Supernatural Woman

The wind of the HOLY SPIRIT is sometimes violent when the LORD shows up. Submit and surrender to the Spirit of the LORD, and don't let sin settle in your heart. This supernatural wind is pushing darkness out of the way of the righteous.

It's impossible for holy revelation and sin to blend; it's like the great gulf, a set fixed place that houses hell and sin. Just ask the rich man who died and went to hell. Not only did he see Lazarus, not the Lazarus who JESUS raised from the dead, but the Lazarus who was a beggar at this rich man's gate, but he wanted two things: he wanted Lazarus to dip his finger in water and cool his tongue because he was in agony of hell's fire and he wanted JESUS to send someone to his brothers to warn them about the reality of hell so they would not go there, too.

The HOLY SCRIPTURES testify *Luke 16:19-31:* *"There was a rich man who was dressed in purple and fine linen and lived in luxury every day. At his gate was laid a beggar named Lazarus, covered with sores and longing to eat what fell from the rich man's table. Even the dogs came and licked his sores. "The time came when the beggar died and the angels carried him*

I'm a supernatural woman, serving a supernatural GOD and getting supernatural results!

to Abraham's side. The rich man also died and was buried. In hell, where he was in torment, he looked up and saw Abraham far away, with Lazarus by his side. So he called to him, 'Father Abraham, have pity on me and send Lazarus to dip the tip of his finger in water and cool my tongue, because I am in agony in this fire.' "But Abraham replied, 'Son, remember that in your lifetime you received your good things, while Lazarus received bad things, but now he is comforted here and you are in agony. And besides all this, between us and you a great gulf has been fixed, so that those who want to go from here to you cannot, nor can anyone cross over from there to us.' "He answered, 'Then I beg you, father, send Lazarus to my father's house, for I have five brothers. Let him warn them, so that they will not also come to this place of torment.' "Abraham replied, 'They have Moses and the Prophets; let them listen to them.' " 'No, father Abraham,' he said, 'but if someone from the dead goes to them, they will repent.' "He said to him, 'If they do not listen to Moses and the Prophets, they will not be convinced even if someone rises from the dead."

None of this was possible after the fact says the LORD, because of the holy distinction between heaven and hell. It's impossible for HOLY revelation and sin to blend. For the first time the rich man showed concern for others. The rich man had failed to pay attention to the HOLY SCRIPTURES and feared his brothers would do the same. If a person's heart is closed and rejects the HOLY SCRIPTURE, no evidence, not even of the resurrection of JESUS CHRIST, will change him.

I'm a supernatural woman, serving a supernatural GOD and getting supernatural results!

I AM arranging MY HOLY agenda in the hearts of MY people in order to establish it in the earth, says the LORD. The hour has come where holy distinction has a mighty voice, establishing MY HOLY choice, says the LORD. When you as a supernatural woman find rest in your hearts because you submit your hearts to ME, the HOLY distinction that is now in the land will be MY voice emanating from your voice, says the LORD.

I the TRUE and LIVING GOD is the only ONE who knows the heart. I created the heart says the LORD. The heart has supernatural functions; the human heart is considered as the center or source of emotions, personality, and attributes or qualities. The heart embodies the inmost thought and feeling: consciousness or conscience. It's the source of emotions contrasted with the mind, the source of intellect or one's emotional nature. The heart establishes one's disposition and any of various humane feelings like love, devotion, sympathy, and moods; all emanate supernaturally from the heart.

Supernatural Tips for the Supernatural Woman

Be careful what you feel, feelings can fool you when you are not being real. Don't let your feelings dictate your outcome. Only GOD knows the heart, surrender your heart to GOD. HIS HOLY SPIRIT will lead you into clarity and victory.

The HOLY SCRIPTURES testifies how the Prophet Jeremiah by the Spirit of GOD, continues to describe the heart as being deceitful above all things

I'm a supernatural woman, serving a supernatural GOD and getting supernatural results!

and beyond cure, who can understand it but GOD. The account picks up in ***Jeremiah 17:9-10*** *"The heart is deceitful above all things and beyond cure. Who can understand it? "I the LORD search the heart and examine the mind, to reward a man according to his conduct, according to what his deeds deserve."* The LORD calling HIS righteous remnant to live in a place where their hearts are no longer deceiving them because HE is constantly revealing in them the holy distinction between righteousness and wickedness. The LORD has to search our heart and examine our mind to reward us according to our conduct and judge us according to what our deeds deserve. When we as supernatural women seek HIM with our whole hearts, and agree with HIS examination, our rewards will be unbelievable. GOD is not a man that HE should lie. HE swore by HIMSELF and will not go against HIS Holy Word, and it will not return back to HIM void. What HE says must show anything else must go.

Supernatural Tips for the Supernatural Woman

The LORD releases HIS supernatural revelation for every situation, and if our heart is pure we will be able to see from GOD'S perspective and wait patiently on the full manifestation of HIS revelation.

As supernatural women, the LORD has invited us into new resting places in HIM whereby HE will cause us to see like never before. There are things HE wants to show us about WHO HE is to us and who we are to HIM, which we could have never attain without HIS supernatural revelation.

I'm a supernatural woman, serving a supernatural GOD and getting supernatural results!

As I have revealed MYSELF to you, says the LORD, I'VE also had to and will continue to expose yourself to you. It's impossible for you to come before ME and I not show you yourself. It's what you do with what I'VE exposed to you, about you, which will determine how much I, the TRUE and LIVING GOD will allow you to see. Holy supernatural revelation exposes all imitation and reveals your limitation, based on what you do with the supernatural information that I release in your spirit. Don't let ME have to say in your final day, depart because of your heart, says the LORD.

The HOLY SCRIPTURES testify of what the Psalmist said in ***Psalm 119:1-12***: *"Blessed are they whose ways are blameless, who walk according to the law of the LORD. Blessed are they who keep his statutes and seek him with all their heart. They do nothing wrong; they walk in his ways. You have laid down precepts that are to be fully obeyed. Oh, that my ways were steadfast in obeying your decrees! Then I would not be put to shame when I consider all your commands. I will praise you with an upright heart as I learn your righteous laws. I will obey your decrees; do not utterly forsake me. How can a young man keep his way pure? By living according to your word. I seek you with all my heart; do not let me stray from your commands. I have hidden your word in my heart that I might not sin against you. Praise be to you, O LORD; teach me your decrees."*

Seeking ME with your whole heart in this hour requires that when you come into MY presence, you humble yourself, says the LORD. Don't come to

ME says the LORD, blaming others. Come to ME inquiring of you and after MY examination of your heart and mind and your receptivity of what I'M showing you about yourself, says the LORD; then you will be able to operate in this HOLY distinction that I released in the land.

Supernatural Tips for the Supernatural Woman

Where there is a limitation because of pretense and imitation, the revelatory information from MY HOLY examination won't benefit you, if you choose to remain in your deceptive situation, says the LORD.

MY HOLY SPIRIT within you enables you or permits you to see the imitation of demonic activity that will become a limitation for you. It's impossible for holy revelation and sin to blend. Remember what looks clean to you, says the LORD, is not necessarily clean to ME. I, the TRUE and LIVING GOD is the only ONE who knows the heart. I need your whole heart to fully impart this holy distinction that is in the land in this hour. Let ME cover you with MY love where the power of MY shed blood washes away all sin and shame.

Chapter 10

A Transformed You Living in the Supernatural New

Romans 12:1-2.
Therefore, I urge you, brothers, in view of God's mercy, to offer your bodies as living sacrifices, holy and pleasing to God this is your spiritual act of worship. Do not conform any longer to the pattern of this world, but be transformed by the renewing of your mind. Then you will be able to test and approve what God's will is his good, pleasing and perfect will.

The Prophetic-Poetic Word
Momentary awakenings of Godly revelations
are normal to the righteous during their daily walk.
The righteous operate by the leading of the Holy Spirit,
where through obedience they are led even when they
should talk.

I'm a supernatural woman, serving a supernatural GOD and getting supernatural results!

The dwelling of the righteous is in the secret place of the most high,
it's an invitation into that holy place where demonic tricks are not tried.
It's that place where GOD'S supernatural sovereignty satisfies their soul,
it's that place of having access to HIS riches untold.

It's where holiness serves as a supernatural reflector,
it's where our level of discernment serves as a supernatural protector.
It's graduating from fleshly reactions,
and not being seduced by negative attractions.

Only the righteous can experience GOD's transforming power,
It's only CHRIST through us where we can experience the supernatural new in this hour.

A Transformed You Living in the Supernatural New

I, the LORD and GOD of the righteous, say: I have ushered you across enemy lines. I command that you wake up to this supernaturally reality as the transformed you, living in the supernatural new. MY HOLY SCRIPTURES testify in *2 Corinthians 5:17: "Therefore, if anyone is in Christ, he is a new creation; the old has gone, the new has come!"* It is time to walk naturally in the realm of the supernatural says the LORD. It's that place where there is a constant awakening of GODLY revelation. I desire to reveal WHO I am to you wherever you are. In the supernatural new, MY moment-by-moment revelation, relative to your present situation, will cause you to answer with GODLY wisdom, escape from traps, and remain on assignment while being led by MY HOLY SPIRIT, says the LORD. MY HOLY SPIRIT will announce answers, give direction, and lead you and guide you into all truth. MY HOLY SCRIPTURES testify in the book of **Isaiah** where the Prophet Isaiah prophesied about the announcement of the new in *Isaiah 42:9 "See, the former things have taken place, and new things I declare; before they spring into being I announce them to you."*

Supernatural Tips for the Supernatural Woman

The supernatural new, is the picture of the daily walk for the transformed you, walking in momentary

I'm a supernatural woman, serving a supernatural GOD and getting supernatural results!

awakenings of GODLY daily revelations. Open your eyes and don't let life take you by surprise.

The Apostle Paul captures this revelation and made every attempt to communicate this to the Church that the transformed mind is a process and not a single event. The HOLY SCRIPTURES testify in the book of **Romans** how the Apostle Paul draws an important reference from the truth set forth about God's mercy and our bodies as holy and living sacrifices unto GOD. This positions the righteous to experience the transformed you, living in the supernatural new. The righteous are to live, in the sense of having the new supernatural life of the HOLY SPIRIT in them as their daily spiritual activity or act. This should not be done out of ritual, but our supernatural reality of a constant activity involving the heart, mind and will in worship to GOD, daily operating in HIS obedient service.

The spiritual transformation just described has taken place, relative to what GOD wants from the believer right now, leads to our spiritual and moral growth being pleasing to GOD, where no improvement can be made on the perfect will of God. The biblical account of the Apostle Paul's letter picks up in ***Romans 12:1-2:*** *"Therefore, I urge you, brothers, in view of God's mercy, to offer your bodies as living sacrifices, holy and pleasing to God this is your spiritual act of worship. Do not conform any longer to the pattern of this world, but be transformed by the renewing of your mind. Then you will be able to test and approve what God's will is his good, pleasing and perfect will."*

Think it not strange that Hollywood came out with a mega film called *The Transformers.* These man-made machines would transform into what they needed to transform into, relative to their needed purpose, based on their present circumstance. The storyline didn't start with Hollywood; it started in Heaven before the foundations of the world when the HOLY TRINITY divinely orchestrated the trans-formed mind. The transformed mind, which is the CHRIST MIND, is activated in the believer at their confession of salvation in JESUS CHRIST as LORD of their lives. This supernatural impartation brings full activation. As the believer obeys the renewal instructions documented by the Apostle Paul, the transformed mind, the already-activated MIND OF CHRIST in us, begins to consume the natural mind of the believer through obedience to CHRIST. This prepares the believer to respond to any and every situation or circumstance manifesting before them without being defeated.

Supernatural Tips for the Supernatural Woman

GOD informs the transformed. As we master allowing the CHRIST mind to override our natural minds through obedience to CHRIST and HIS HOLY WORD, moment by moment and second by second, knowledge, insight, wisdom, and the might of the LORD is ignited in our spirit. In other words, what's already in us is supernaturally made available to us.

I tell MY supernatural woman this day, says the LORD, when it's time to come up higher, I'LL invite you in if there is no sin. I'LL invite you higher when you refuse to sup with the liar. MY secret place is a sacred place and holiness is the supernatural key to insider information in ME. MY HOLY SCRIPTURES testify in *1 Peter 1:15-16: "But just as he who called you is holy, so be holy in all you do; for it is written: "Be holy, because I am holy."* Why would I say be holy as I AM holy says the LORD, so the righteous can dwell where the GREAT I AM already exist. I tell you, says the LORD, the devil can't dwell on every level. Only the chosen and the few have access to the new. I'M looking to inform the transformed.

Come into the supernatural new and let ME talk to you, says the LORD…Remember that MY HOLY SCRIPTURES testify in *1 Peter 2:9-10: "But you are a chosen people, a royal priesthood, a holy nation, a people belonging to God, that you may declare the praises of him who called you out of darkness into his wonderful light. Once you were not a people, but now you are the people of God; once you had not received mercy, but now you have received mercy."* In the season of the supernatural new, MY righteous remnant must seek a holy satisfaction for their souls that can only come from sanctification by truth.

Supernatural Tips for the Supernatural Woman

No sanctification, no holy revelation.
MY HOLY SCRIPTURES testify in **John 17** how I prayed to MY Father while I was still in the world where MY disciples are to do their work; I, JESUS, did not wish for them to be taken from the world until that work is done. I told MY Father, as you sent ME, I have sent them. MY preordained mission

I'm a supernatural woman, serving a supernatural GOD and getting supernatural results!

is given as the pattern for MY followers, says the LORD. You may long for heaven, but it is on earth that your work is done, says the LORD. I asked MY FATHER, sanctify them by truth; your WORD is truth. Sanctification and holy revelation go together. It is the connection between holiness and truth, says the LORD. A satisfied sanctified soul loves truth; if you love truth, you love ME because I AM TRUTH. The more you obey the truth, the more I'LL show you how to live within the guidelines of truth through MY revelation.

In other words, I'LL show you how to work out what I'VE already worked in you, says the LORD. I sanctified myself that they too may be sanctified, says the LORD, "setting MYSELF apart to do MY FATHER'S will," which at this point for ME meant MY death. I died on the cross not only to save and establish eternal life, but also to enable and to empower you to be consecrated to GOD'S service, says the LORD.

The account picks up where MY HOLY SCRIPTURES testify in *John 17:15-19: "My prayer is not that you take them out of the world but that you protect them from the evil one. They are not of the world, even as I am not of it. Sanctify them by the truth; your word is truth. As you sent me into the world, I have sent them into the world. For them I sanctify myself, that they too may be truly sanctified."* No sanctification, no holy revelation. Remember, momentary awakenings of Godly revelations are normal to the righteous during their daily walk. We are also supplied with levels of discernment, which

I'm a supernatural woman, serving a supernatural GOD and getting supernatural results!

provides supernatural protection. It's where the supernatural reflector, called holiness, serves as the supernatural detector and protector that secures the borders of the righteous.

Supernatural Tips for the Supernatural Woman

The transformed you living in the supernatural new is where the satisfied, sanctified soul is easily led by the LORD. When we live within the perimeters and boundaries of HIS glory it's easy to surrender our story for HIS perspective. Our confession of HIS LORDSHIP in our lives grants us the power to rule and reign with HIM in this hour.

Chapter 11

SUPERNATURALLY SPEAKING, NO PERMISSION IS NEEDED

Mark 14:6-9

Leave her alone," said Jesus. "Why are you bothering her? She has done a beautiful thing to me. The poor you will always have with you, and you can help them any time you want. But you will not always have me. She did what she could. She poured perfume on my body beforehand to prepare for my burial. I tell you the truth, wherever the gospel is preached throughout the world, what she has done will also be told, in memory of her."

The Prophetic-Poetic Word
Permission is never needed in Christ,
because a surrendered will always has access to an open door.

I'm a supernatural woman, serving a supernatural GOD and getting supernatural results!

Revelation and clarity comes through holiness and obedience,
this supernaturally ushers the righteous into what existed before.

There is no permission need, says the LORD, when you are easily led by MY Spirit,
it's that place where a holy invitation welcomes us into new dimensions.
There is always access to realms of glory,
where through CHRIST we monitor our heart intensions.

What others say or do, says the LORD, can't stop us,
because the righteous are determined to follow ME.
Distractions from demonic realms can't hold our attention,
because of MY goodness, says the LORD, I'VE given the righteous eyes to see.

There is a place in ME, says the LORD, where no permission needed,
it's where freedom in Christ there is a supernatural no restriction zone.
When what's precious to the righteous is given up for the LORD,
there is no excuse for HIM not to call the righteous HIS own.

Supernaturally Speaking, No Permission is Needed

The LORD is saying to HIS righteous remnant, *No permission needed*, is a pre-ordained position than can only be attained through CHRIST that permits the righteous to live and supernaturally operate in no restriction zones in the spirit. This is a supernatural realm of glory where the same authority that the FATHER gave the SON is made manifest for HIS righteous remnant. *No permission needed* grants the righteous supernatural authority and access to live in the manifested fullness of CHRIST and experience what already exist for them. It's where nothing can bother you, says the LORD, because I already told it to leave you alone.

Mark 14:6 *"Leave her alone," said Jesus. "Why are you bothering her? She has done a beautiful thing to me."* I told the hecklers and false accusers to leave her alone, says the LORD, because I did not want them to hinder her preordained moment. They couldn't see it, but I already knew what she had to do. She didn't even understand why she felt the intense pursuit to head towards ME, but she was supernaturally empowered by the reverence and love that she had in her heart for ME, says the LORD. I tell you this day, says the TRUE and LIVING GOD, when you love ME and reverence ME, nothing can stop you from getting to ME.

Supernatural Tips for the Supernatural Woman

Love has the power will lift you up higher than the realm of the liar and escort you into destiny.

I will remember you. When you remember ME says the LORD, anything or anyone who is trying to hinder your access from getting to ME, don't worry about it, I have already blocked them. Where no permission is needed, says the LORD, not every spirit can get through. Think it not strange, says the LORD, anytime that you purpose in your heart as a supernatural woman to do anything for ME, by the time you put it into action, opposition will be there to try to stop you. The enemy will use voices and other people's choice to harass the righteous and influence them, so as not to do what they want to do for ME. Love will lift you up higher than the realm of the liar where no permission is needed. Believe this day that love has already cleared the path of the righteous, says the LORD.

When you press through to do what you need to do for ME, says the LORD, you supernaturally break through to the other side of opposition. On the other side of opposition there is no resistance because there is no law against love. It's that place where *no permission needed* grants the righteous access to ME. It's called supernatural obedience because those who love ME obey ME. It where the righteous can please ME all they want to because I have blocked all opposition, says the LORD. Anything that you do in ME, through ME, or unto ME, says the LORD, is what I call "a beautiful and unforgettable thing."

I'm a supernatural woman, serving a supernatural GOD and getting supernatural results!

No permission needed in CHRIST is where a surrendered life has the capacity to move with a supernatural liberty in the spirit as well as in the natural because that life has grown or developed into a place where it supernaturally understands the perimeters and the boundaries of GOD'S glory. Anytime, in any place, and anywhere the righteous don't need permission is a place where they have been cleared by CHRIST for full access, because they are willing to surrender their precious thing.

The HOLY SCRIPTURES testify in *Mark 14:7: "The poor you will always have with you, and you can help them any time you want. But you will not always have me."* There are times in life where we can bless the poor anytime that we want to because they will always be around as long as time exist, but at the same time JESUS was saying don't stop her from giving to ME what is precious to her. If you took this precious thing and sold it, even the money gained from the sale of this precious thing would not be enough or have the capacity to meet all the needs of the poor.

JESUS was saying don't get in her way. You can't see it, but this supernatural woman was given permission before the foundations of the world to step into MY destiny; to prepare for MY burial. I tell you this day, says the TRUE and LIVING GOD, you always have access to destiny; you just need permission to get there. When you surrender your precious thing, permission is granted. Anything that you hold on to that means more to you than ME will hinder your preordained destiny. There are some people, places, and things that can't walk with you in destiny. You can't walk close with those who are still looking for man's approval and not GOD'S permission. GOD'S permission is gained through love, reverence, holiness, righteousness, and obedience.

Supernatural Tips for the Supernatural Woman

When GOD is calling you to do something, permission already left HIS throne. Push pass the crowd to surrender to GOD what's precious to you. Don't let someone else's no determine your destiny.

When I, the TRUE AND LIVING GOD, grant the righteous permission in ME, don't ever allow someone else's no to stop you. The supernatural reality is, only if you let them they can. Where no permission is needed, you can't even stop to acknowledge darkness. The enemy will distract you in order to attack you. This is not a season to make excuses when it comes to serving GOD. It is imperative that we walk blameless before the LORD. This supernatural, no restriction zone is a blameless zone. It's that place where submission unto the LORD repositions us in HIM to be granted permission by HIM.

The HOLY SCRIPTURES continue to testify in **Mark 14:8:** *"She did what she could. She poured perfume on my body beforehand to prepare for my burial"*. This woman did what she could do because she loved ME says the LORD. Whenever you love ME more than those who are trying to stop you from doing what you need to do for ME, you will have the supernatural power to push pass them to obey ME.

I'm a supernatural woman, serving a supernatural GOD and getting supernatural results!

Just as this woman demonstrated her love for ME, says the LORD, little did she know by doing what she could do, it was the preordained timeslot for her to do it, says the LORD. Those who say they love ME will have the opportunity to do the same.

As you demonstrate your love to ME through obedience, I will position you within time to walk into your destiny. When you surrender your precious thing, anything or anyone who is trying to hinder your access from getting to ME, remember I have already supernaturally blocked them by MY SPIRIT says the LORD

Supernatural Tips for the Supernatural Woman

Do what you can do, and GOD will move everything else out of your way.

The LORD is saying that "no permission needed" is a supernatural place where false accusations from the enemy's camp no longer affect the righteous because their hearing is keenly adjusted to the SHEPHERD'S voice. The righteous can move with a supernatural ease through realms and dimensions because demonic traps can't hold the righteous or their attention. Where no permission is needed. The eyes of your heart are enlightened. This means that your mind or understanding or inner awareness is charged and alert relative to who you are and WHOSE you are.

When this woman poured perfume on MY body beforehand to prepare for my burial, says the LORD, she knew something more. Because of Jewish customs, this woman knew about anointing

I'm a supernatural woman, serving a supernatural GOD and getting supernatural results!

the body before burial, but there was a supernatural understanding that she had that others around her couldn't see. Her obedience documented her destiny in the HOLY SCRIPTURES. She did not have a clue about how the Apostle Paul would take it to another level, describing a fragrance: how the Christian, who experiences spiritual warfare and who is triumphantly led by GOD in CHRIST and through CHRIST that God spreads everywhere the "fragrance" of the knowledge of CHRIST. The HOLY SCRIPTURES testify in *2 Corinthians 2:14-15: "But thanks be to God, who always leads us in triumphal procession in Christ and through us spreads everywhere the fragrance of the knowledge of him. For we are to God the aroma of Christ among those who are being saved and those who are perishing."* Apostle Paul describes an immensely rich outpouring of triumphant faith in praise of the unfailing adequacy of the grace of God for every conceivable situation, no matter how threatening and destructive it may seem to be, leads us in triumphal procession.

As a supernatural woman in the midst of opposition, because of our submission to CHRIST, there is a scent or fragrance we must carry, that others can smell through the aroma of our testimony that repositions us in CHRIST where no permission is needed to proceed in supernatural victorious outcomes. So whatever, whenever, and wherever you do anything in ME, through ME or unto ME, says the LORD, you will never be forgotten by ME. When you are not ashamed of ME, I won't be ashamed of you. Remember, I'VE already chosen you and given you the authority to

I'm a supernatural woman, serving a supernatural GOD and getting supernatural results!

carry MY fragrance. There is no permission needed for those who carry my fragrance says the LORD.

The HOLY SCRIPTURES testify in *John 10:17-18* *"the reason my Father loves me is that I lay down my life only to take it up again. No one takes it from me, but I lay it down of my own accord. I have authority to lay it down and authority to take it up again. This command I received from my Father."* The LORD is saying to us this day that the love of GOD that is WHO HE is, is so powerful that it positions the righteous in a supernatural realm of authority. They do not need permission to operate and navigate in dimensions and realms in the spirit, and anything in the spirit that operates beneath love must get permission from them. *No permission needed*, grants the righteous supernatural authority and access to live in the manifested fullness of CHRIST and experience what already exist for them. It's where nothing can bother you, says the LORD, because I already told it to leave you alone.

Supernatural Tips for the Supernatural Woman

The fragrance of CHRIST on our lives coupled with the supernatural authority that we have been given through CHRIST, positions us as supernatural women to experience continuous manifested victories.

CPSIA information can be obtained at www.ICGtesting.com
Printed in the USA
BVOW11s1128220315

392754BV00003B/5/P

9 781628 712018